THE MIRACLE MAN

T0347505

Douglas Maxwell

THE MIRACLE MAN

OBERON BOOKS
LONDON

First published in 2010 by Oberon Books Ltd
521 Caledonian Road, London N7 9RH
Tel: 020 7607 3637 / Fax: 020 7607 3629
e-mail: info@oberonbooks.com
www.oberonbooks.com

Copyright © Douglas Maxwell 2010

Douglas Maxwell is hereby identified as author of this play in accordance with section 77 of the Copyright, Designs and Patents Act 1988. The Author has asserted his moral rights.

All rights whatsoever in this play are strictly reserved and application for performance etc. should be made before commencement of rehearsal to United Agents, 12-26 Lexington Street, London W1F OLE. No performance may be given unless a licence has been obtained, and no alterations may be made in the title or the text of the play without the Author's prior written consent.

This book is sold subject to the condition that it shall not by way of trade or otherwise be circulated without the publisher's consent in any form of binding or cover or circulated electronically other than that in which it is published and without a similar condition including this condition being imposed on any subsequent purchaser.

A catalogue record for this book is available from the British Library.

ISBN: 978-1-84943-032-6

Cover image by Jesse Tise

The Miracle Man was first performed at the Tron Theatre, Glasgow in a National Theatre of Scotland production, on the 10th March 2010, with the following cast:

Ross Allan	Chubb
Shabana Bakhsh	Fawziya
Charlene Boyd	Dawn
Jimmy Chisholm	Healy & Lewis
Keith Fleming	Ozzy
Sally Reid	Paula

Creative Team

Douglas Maxwell	Writer
Vicky Featherstone	Director
Georgia McGuinness	Designer
Natasha Chivers	Lighting Designer
Mark Melville	Sound Designer

Part One

OZZY is lit by stars which flicker and pulse around him.

OZZY: Make it…

Make it that there's this guy.

A guy who feels…like everything he's ever done was wrong. But then, right at the end, it turns out that he…

No that's shite.

Right. There's a guy who feels…so…

Old. Even though he's not. Not that old anyway. But this guy feels like he's carrying the years on his shoulders or something. He feels them digging into his shoulders, like a…schoolbag. He's carrying a weight. He has slumped shoulders this guy, even though he's big. Well, strong. Well. Used to be.

And it's…kind of…terrifying him. This guy lies awake at night. Terrified. The end.

What about that? Is that a story? Do you want that story?

No. Needs a bit more eh?

Okay. Right. Right…one afternoon, like tea time, he's on his way back to Central Station and he passes the queue for The Cathouse. And all the kids are there waiting to get in, cold and squealing. Buzzing, trying to look easy. It's an under-age disco – probably not called a disco but you know what I mean. They're really young, queued up. And he's looking at all these kids, thinking that they all look ridiculous now, and kind of, unrecognisable. All this hugging and touching each other's hair and laughing and jumping and hugging – it's unrecognisable really.

But something about the way they are, the way they're standing or they way they laugh reminds him of…a forgotten thing. An important thing. And although he, kind of, can't explain it, in words, he can taste it. He knows he wants it. God – Jesus Christ he wants whatever that is. To be one of them. To be how they are. What they are. Right now.

But he wants so many impossible things doesn't he, this guy? So it takes him by surprise.

It takes him by surprise when out of the blue, suddenly… he gets what he wants.

He turns young. He turns 15 again. Right there outside The Cathouse. He transforms.

And it's like a miracle.

No-one tells you that you can choose your age. You can be any age you want to be, but no-one tells you that.

As he goes down the queue he gets younger and younger. His ancient tracksuit gets slack on his shoulders, his eyes brighten, everything brightens. And he joins onto the end of the queue. Just joins in. Just like that. He remembers.

And it's all…just…good…just really good. Until…

Until the bouncer sees him.

"What age are you? Under 15s! What's the game?" And folk are looking and…yeah…

Well. That's it. Adult suspicion. The spell is broken. It's the dead-eyed suspicion from the people in the street that ends it. He sees what they see and…

Miracle over.

He tries to speak but his voice breaks. He makes a lunge for the door but his bones buckle. He hits the floor heavy – just like a middle aged man.

He grows old again.

And before he knows it he's…I dunno…running I suppose. In and out of traffic. All the way home. Running home. Racing for his life.

And when he gets home he…feels…he can't…he just can't hold it in anymore. He can't hold in all this fucking pain anymore, it has to explode, it has to, it has to explode or he'll burn to bits in this blue, horrible light. It has to explode so it does, and when it comes it keeps on coming and he lets it explode right past him and it is an explosion and it's correct, it's correct it really is correct and he smashes up the flat, the whole fucking place trashed, smashed and pounding and smashing the fucking glass and pulling down the fucking pictures and ripping the precious books and grabbing the curtains and punching himself in the chest and punching, punching, punching himself in the chest and…

Crying.

Until it's…just

Smithereens.

And he takes off his clothes. And he lies on the floor. And he pulls up his knees and puts his thumb in his mouth and

It's funny, this guy thinks. No-one tells you that you can choose your age. You can be any age you want to be, but no-one tells you that. We just plod on in chronological order. So this is the age I'll be now. I think. I want to be this age now.

He tries to picture his father's face, but he can't. He tries to imagine being cradled. But he can't.

It feels like a generation ago that they took his dad back into hospital, but it was only this morning. He got the call when he was on his way back to Central Station, heading home.

"You need to prepare yourself for the end pet", the nurse had said.

So maybe that's what this is all about?

Maybe that's why he's lying there, in smithereens, like a newborn, in broken glass.

Waiting.

What about that?

No.

That's…

Unbelievable. That would never happen.

No-one would do that. No-one would even want to do that.

So instead…

Make it

That when the call comes in, the guy just does what he's told to do. He always does what he's told to do this guy. He keeps walking. He gets to Central, gets on a different train. Then a bus. And he comes out to the hospital. Like he was told to do. And he waits where he's told to wait. And sits where he's told to sit. And he follows her down the corridor, just like he was told to do.

And when he's told that they'll be left alone and that he should speak, even though in real life, they never spoke, not really…well, that's just what he does.

What about that? Is that a story? Do you want that story?

***

We can see now that OZZY is sitting in a darkened hospital room, the stars are just the blinking lights on the equipment hooked up to the bed beside him.

*OZZY's a big man. He used to be fit. He's wearing a tracksuit.
He's in his mid-thirties/early forties.*

*An old man lies unconscious in the bed. This is LEWIS
MacDonald, OZZY's dad.*

*OZZY's chest is sore. God it feels like he really hurt himself there,
punching like that. He undoes the buttons on his shirt and there's
a bruise right enough. Right in the middle of his chest. Right
where he was pounding during the story. Or is the bruise from
before, when he really…? Well, whatever, it's sore.*

*He's rubbing the bruise with his eyes shut when a nurse, PAULA,
enters.*

*OZZY guiltily does up the buttons on his shirt like a cheating lover
caught in the act. Did she hear him? How long has she been at the
door? Should he say something or…?*

*She gives him no clues as she goes about tenderly checking LEWIS
and the IV drip.*

*Nah, she couldn't have heard him. She would say wouldn't she?
People don't normally narrate stories in hospital rooms do they,
she would mention it, wouldn't she?*

*Regardless, OZZY is stewing in his own juices as she leaves. Just as
he thinks he's got away with it…*

PAULA: Oh, and Ozzy. You know what's good for sore chests?
Not doing this…

PAULA pantomimes OZZY beating his chest in full dramatic fury.

PAULA: Cheeribye!

*She gives him a wee wink to let him know she's only taking the piss
and then she's gone.*

OZZY's frozen.

The door opens again and PAULA pokes her head round.

PAULA: I liked it by the way. Your wee story. It was good.

She gives him the thumbs up.

Zombie-like, OZZY returns the gesture.

***

The school bell rings. The kids pour through the gates, as does OZZY carrying both a brief case and a sports hold-all.

Parting the crowd like a superstar is DAWN. She must be fifteen but looks a lot older in her school stuff. She's white, obviously affluent and super-confident. She moves in the upper echelons of the playground ranks.

FAWZIYA stops stuffing crisps into her gub for a moment as DAWN passes. FAWZIYA is an Asian girl of the same age. She wears a blue Jilbab (a loose, ankle length gown) and a head scarf or Hijab. Something about the way she drops her eyes when DAWN catwalks past tells us that they don't exactly move in the same circles. Actually just being near to DAWN makes FAWZIYA feel fat...well...fatter.

Attempting the same attention grabbing entrance through the crowd is Robert CHUBB. He too sports confidence, swagger and a superior, cheesy grin, but this time absolutely no-one reacts. Well, they might groan and turn away as he clicks his fingers and points hello to confused first years. Not that he notices this daily mass rejection. He has a great deal of thick skin, does CHUBB. CHUBB is under the impression that he's a mover and shaker in the school, despite large amounts of evidence to the contrary.

A crowd forms a circle around DAWN, drawn by an impressive sparkling item of jewellery on her wedding finger.

A ring.

A ring that catches the light and dazzles everyone.

Oh this old thing? Well, there's a story to this....

The second bell sweeps them all away. FAWZIYA is the last to leave. She shuffles after them sadly.

***

Lunchtime in the Gym Hall and OZZY is trying to set up a poster about food groups on a flip chart. There's a circle of seats with only two taken.

Sitting far apart from each other are FAWZIYA and CHUBB. FAWZIYA has her head down trying her best to be invisible, while CHUBB is trying, and succeeding, not to be.

CHUBB: There's no-one else coming. It's already a tepid failure and it's not even twenty to one, first day of the club.

OZZY: Give it time. The bell's just gone.

CHUBB: No point. If Jamie Oliver couldn't do it, you've no chance.

OZZY: Well you two are here aren't you, so that's something.

CHUBB: It's a failure is what it is. Ozzy, can I come to your house one day?

OZZY: What? No.

CHUBB: How not? I won't stay long, just check it out, cup of tea. It'll be like Cribs.

OZZY: Absolutely not. And don't call me Ozzy either.

CHUBB: How not?

OZZY: Cos I'm a teacher.

CHUBB: A PE teacher.

OZZY: And Guidance.

CHUBB: Mr Healy said all PE teachers are dumb-dumbs.

OZZY: No he didn't.

CHUBB: Did. He says he's got all the dumb-dumbs wrapped round his little finger. And he says Techy teachers are violent paranoids who are out to get him. Janice lets me call her by her first name and I've been outside her house hunners of times.

OZZY: Who's Janice?

CHUBB: Janice McManus. Religious Studies.

OZZY: Mrs McManus' name is Alma.

CHUBB: Is it? Oh. That explains why she didn't look round when I was shouting through her window. Just sat on her couch inhaling a macaroni pie straight from the poke. God I feel bad about all that other stuff I shouted now. She was pretty frightened by the end. Ozzy, can I make a speech?

OZZY: Eh?

CHUBB: May I address the group?

OZZY: No. And you've to call me Mr MacDonald. Right, let's get started. Fawziya, have you brought in your lunch for us to discuss?

FAWZIYA has a Tupperware tub and a bottle of orange juice that she hands over.

CHUBB: I haven't brought mine and I'll tell you for why...

OZZY: Brown bread, good. An apple. That's a portion right there. As is the orange juice unless you've had some already. Have you had any other fruit juice today?

CHUBB: It's irrelevant.

FAWZIYA shakes her head.

OZZY: What's in the sandwich...what is it? Is it...curry?

CHUBB: Ooooooh. Racist.

OZZY: No! It is curry isn't it? Chicken curry?

FAWZIYA shakes her head.

CHUBB: *(Sucking in his breath through his teeth.)* This is a mess. A poorly attended, racist mess.

FAWZIYA says something that no-one can hear/understand.

OZZY: Oh right. Very good. Tasty. See, we're…learning. Well…let's move on.

He hands back the Tupperware.

CHUBB: I'm worried that you're not suited to this Ozzy. You're a fish out of water. And how come it's you that's doing this healthy eating group anyway and not somebody good? What's food got to do with P.E?

OZZY: P.E. is a broad church.

CHUBB: Healy forced you into it didn't he? He made you do this cos everyone else told him to ram it.

OZZY: *(Yes.)* No. Not at all. That's not true. No, no, no. This is a very important issue and I'm more than happy to step up. History is made by those who take action. Remember that. Grand gestures change the world. I'm a do-er.

CHUBB: That's not what Mr Healy called you. He said he made you do this and he could make you do much worse.

OZZY: No he did not.

CHUBB: And look, obviously we all pity you a wee bit, so let me do you a favour here and cut to the chase. It doesn't matter what you eat. That's what my speech is about. It's irrelevant.

OZZY: The group is going to discuss this Chubb, that's the whole…

CHUBB: Ah ha! Case closed. No more further questions m'lud.

OZZY: Eh?

CHUBB: You called me Chubb.

OZZY: That's your name, Robert Chubb.

CHUBB: Aye, Robert Chubb. Robert. But who calls me that? No-one. Robert: a name with about a thousand shortenings; Bob, Bobby, Rob, Robbie, Bert, Bertie...

OZZY: Okay, I'll call you Bertie if you shut your face and let us get on with the food groups in Fawziya's Tupperware.

CHUBB: What I'm trying to say is it doesnae matter what's in the Tupperware if you've got a fat name. Chubb's a fat name, as is, I'm sorry to say, Fawziya. Thinking about it, Alma's a fat name too, which explains the macaroni pie dinner for one.

OZZY: What are you talking about?

CHUBB: We've got no choice! It's our destiny to be feasters. It's fate. It's all in the name. All I'm saying is, we're each of us heading for a pre-destined end: fat, thin, hairy, bald, hero, villain. And you can't fight it. But you can look for clues to prepare yourself. It might be your name, it might be coincidences, deja vu, anything. Like, I've got the vertigo right? 'Member that time I shat myself at Butlins? I'm pretty sure that's cos I'm destined to die by plummeting into a gaping abyss or something. So, armed with that information, every time I go near an abyss, or a potential abyss, I always act with great dignity, making a memorable speech to passers by just in case I get promoted to glory. I'm prepared for the end. Are you? Doubt it. You've got to ask yourself: "Where are the clues to my fate?" "How will I end up?"

OZZY: Chubb? Maybe you should give this group a by eh?

CHUBB: How?

OZZY: Because you're an unsettling element. Go and hang out with your pals.

OZZY tries again to set up the poster.

CHUBB: *(Quieter.)* Naw. Naw you're alright. I'll be quiet I promise. *(Beat.)* Lunchtime Clubs are the future. I join them all, even the crappy ones like this. I've started one actually. It's called The Legion of Legendary Questers. Or Lolq for short. We're trying to rekindle the spirit of King Arthur's court every Friday in the music cupboard. We've got helmets. We're all on a quest and it's ripping me man. First one to complete the quest takes over the entire club: for three generations. Horny Connelly says he's nearly done it and I've no even started yet. I refuse to let that wee Lord of The Rings-obsessed fannypad push my club into the piss poor realm of fantasy fiction. See me, I'm all about where myth meets reality. Not bloody…Orcs. Ozzy, see next week, can I give a talk on healthy eating in the age of the dragon?

FAWZIYA: Fawziya isn't my real name.

CHUBB: Eh?

FAWZIYA: My real name isn't Fawziya. It's Gale. I took the name Fawziya when I came back to Islam.

OZZY: Well there you go. Brilliant, see. That just shows you. You can change your…fate or whatever. Good for you Fawziya. To be perfectly honest I think that's great, I really do.

CHUBB: I've got a bit of bad news.

OZZY: What?

CHUBB: Gale's a fat name too.

DAWN bustles in. Before they've had time to realise what they've done, all the others have stood. This doesn't bother DAWN in the least.

DAWN: Oh my God I'm sorry I'm like, a hundred years late or something. I just saw the poster a minute ago and I'm like that, I am there. So I'm here. *(To FAWZIYA.)* Hiya!

That's a first. It stuns FAWZIYA. Her Tupperware squirts out of her hand like a bar of soap and she has to chase it across the floor.

OZZY: Right. Well. Good. Have a seat. I believe you'll get a chair there next to Bertie.

CHUBB: *(To DAWN.)* Alright? Robert Chubb. Mind we were in that play together? Not together but…I was very much in the room. You can call me Rob. Or Robbie. Or Reblin The Wondrous.

DAWN: Oh aye. Chubb. You shat yourself at Butlins didn't you?

CHUBB: That was fate. As is, perhaps, this. We're running a bit late. Ozzy's struggling to galvanize the group. To be fair to him his hand's been forced and the racism is debatable.

OZZY: Ho! It's Mr MacDonald. One more and you're straight down the corridor to Mr Healy's office. Understand?

DAWN: I just thought like, I'm a total food Nazi right…?

CHUBB: As am I.

DAWN: I'm so picky. Jamie Oliver is a…a…saint to me. Even the smell of MacDonalds gives me the Dry B's. When I saw there's this healthy eating lunchtime club I was like that, no way. This…is destiny or something.

CHUBB: Yes! Destiny. Exactly my word. It's almost like we're on a…a…

DAWN: This is where I should start my campaign! Healthy eating, healthy body. A healthy body is a sanctified body. A sanctified body is a holy body. A holy body is an uncorrupted body. Know what I mean?

A long silence is the answer.

OZZY: What's your name dear?

DAWN: Dawn West.

OZZY: I don't recognize you. You're not in any team or…

DAWN: No way! I do not run. I do not. *(To FAWZIYA.)* Do you? No. We don't run Sir. We do not.

OZZY: Right. Okay Dawn, well, what we're doing here is…

DAWN: Sir can I make a speech?

OZZY: What about?

CHUBB: Oh aye she gets to make a speech!

OZZY: You've made your speech.

CHUBB: In the face of great censorship.

OZZY: What's the speech about Dawn?

DAWN: It's about this.

The ring. It shines unnaturally and captivates the room for a second or two.

DAWN: It's engraved. See what it says? It says M, M, M.

CHUBB: "Mmmmm".

DAWN: What?

CHUBB: Is it pronounced "Mmmmm"?

DAWN: No. It's pronounced M, M, M. It stands for The Miracle Man Movement. You get it when you complete The Pathway.

OZZY: The Pathway?

DAWN: Aye. And at the end of The Pathway you get a ring and a bible. I've loads of leaflets look.

She roots in her bag and produces a fistful of yellow flyers which she hands out.

OZZY: And this is…something to do with the NHS is it?

DAWN: The NHS? No. Gadz.

OZZY: But it's an NHS thing isn't it? The Pathway?

DAWN: Sir, as I've just this minute said: No. Gadz.

OZZY: Wait a minute though. The Pathway is when they take someone who is…you know…in the final stage of the disease or whatever and move him to a pump for the morphine and get rid of the computers and…

DAWN: Sir, it's The Miracle Man! He is like the most amazing thing you have ever seen. He's totally American and he does this massive show, with miracles and hip-hop choirs and R & B preaching and a great big flashing neon cross and it is the most stunning thing that's ever happened ever. It is totally nothing like the NHS. See when you see it, you will literally…die.

CHUBB: Sounds amazing.

DAWN: It is. And that's just the start. See at the end he totally summons up The Howling Abyss…

CHUBB gasps and grabs OZZY.

DAWN: *(Cont.)*…opens his Heart Of Truth to the world and then… *(Screaming.)* BOOOOOOM!…

CHUBB: Ah! Shat myself there…

DAWN: That's when the miracle happens. Boom! Everyone gets their soul cleaned and they're pure and righteous again. The miracle of purity. And everyone that's pure gets a ring. I mean it – a ring.

OZZY: What…is…what…are…wh…?

DAWN: He's only in the UK for two weeks so we have to be speedy! I did The Pathway at my Auntie's church in England when she was having a breakdown and my mum and me went to feed the iguanas. We used to call her Auntie Depressant but then she tried to gas herself in the oven and it wasn't that funny any more.

CHUBB: You can't do that nowadays. They changed the gas. Doesnae work.

DAWN: I know but it makes you spew like mad.

CHUBB: It would do, aye. Doesn't kill you though.

DAWN: No I know, she's not dead.

DAWN gives FAWZIYA an exasperated "this guy's a dick" look.

OZZY: Dawn, just to clear up…has this got anything at all to do with cancer?

DAWN: No! God sake.

OZZY: He doesn't doesn't claim to cure it or anything this Miracle Boy?

DAWN: Eh? Sir, what you on about?

OZZY: I'm just…it all seems…I suppose…what's it got to do with our healthy eating group?

DAWN: *(Long suffering sigh.)* Healthy eating, healthy body, I've told you! Sir we need to get Mr Healy on board as soon as. The Miracle Man says Scotland's got the highest rate of teen pregnancies in Europe and he can't wait to come up here and get stuck in.

OZZY: Stuck in to what?

DAWN: Duh! Sir it's a virginity ring. Everyone that wears this ring is making a pledge to keep their virginity until they get married. That's the whole point of The Miracle Man.

Both FAWZIYA and CHUBB are more than intrigued.

DAWN: Not just sex, but dry humping, Latvian Whistles, everything. Even winching! You're not allowed to do it. Not just for teen pregnancies, but to save us from STDs and date rape and like, the works. *(Completely different voice.)* The greatest gift you can give your beloved on your wedding night is your virginity. Sure it is Sir?

OZZY: Em…look Dawn, I always say that it's best to keep religion out of the PE department. Maybe try Religious Studies.

DAWN: I've tried, but Mrs McManus won't come out the base cos she says she's being stalked.

OZZY and FAWZIYA give CHUBB a look. He shrugs, "what?".

DAWN: *(Cont.)* And anyway, it's not religious. Well it's not totally religious. There's a cross and bibles but he says it's for all religions. *(To FAWZIYA.)* Buddhists and everything. And like, like, Fawziya, you've never even got off with anyone have you? See you'd be brilliant. Oh! I'm like that, brainwave! Fawziya me and you could be Intimacy Partners. Do you want to? Do you? Do you want to Fawziya? Do you?

FAWZIYA: Wh…what does it mean?

DAWN: You do The Pathway and I help you. Then you and me cope with our cravings together. We'd be like best friends or something. That would prove it wasn't religious wouldn't it Sir? Wouldn't it? Do you want to? Fawziya? Do you want to?

FAWZIYA: I…em…All…

DAWN: Yes! Sir you have to ask Mr Healy!

CHUBB: I'm in 'n all. Mark me down as an Intimate Partner. I've got cravings coming out of my nut man.

DAWN: Just us girls.

CHUBB: Aw. I'm gagging for the Miracle Man. The Abyss, miracles, virginity. You're talking my language Dawn I mean it.

DAWN: Sir everyone will think you're brilliant when you get Mr Healy to bring The Miracle Man to the school. We could do it in an assembly. *(That voice again.)* Ask yourself, what makes you special? What makes you unique? What is it about yourself that you prize above all other things?

These questions hang in the air a bit and FAWZIYA and OZZY catch each other's eye as they struggle to come up with an answer. After a moment...

CHUBB: *(Sings.)* "I am beautiful, no-matter what they say! Words can't bring me down" That kind of thing?

DAWN: I think you should do it today sir so you should.

CHUBB: Oh he'll do it today, don't worry about that Dawn. He's a do-er.

OZZY: Wait a minute...

CHUBB: History is made by men like him.

OZZY: What is it you want me to...?

CHUBB: Grand gestures change the world.

OZZY: Chubb shut it a minute. People really want this?

DAWN: Totally. Absolutely totally.

CHUBB: You'll rise above the dumb-dumbs. You'll be your own man for once.

DAWN: You'll be the hero.

Pause.

OZZY: Okay look...okay look – I'll talk to Mr Healy and see if it's...

DAWN: Yes! Here's all the info and that – Fawziya I'll get you at the yellow gate after the bell and you can come over to my bit and we'll get going on the Pathway. Thanks Sir and this was a totally amazing healthy eating club by the way, I feel transformed so I do. Don't you Fawziya?

OZZY: But...

CHUBB: Can I please come to your bit as well Dawn?

DAWN: This is just intimacy partners Chubb, but you'll be totally part of the team right?

CHUBB: The V Team!

DAWN: Eh?

CHUBB: V. V for Virgins.

DAWN: Aye very good.

CHUBB: Yes! The V Team. Oh God yes. I'm…I'm…so in. Anything you need Dawn. Consider me your Knight Errant.

DAWN: *(Warily.)* Right. Good.

Dawn's on her way out. Chubb's getting ready to follow her out.

OZZY: Wait. What about the food groups?

CHUBB: Ach you tried your best Ozzy, but you were only a pawn in their game. *(To DAWN as they're getting the coats on etc.)* Hey, what's he like by the way, The Miracle Man?

DAWN: Oh he's like a normal guy, except he's ace and his heart is growing on the outside.

CHUBB: Eh?

DAWN: His heart's growing on the outside.

CHUBB: Gadz.

DAWN: No it's not disgusting, it's beautiful. It's the prophesy. A man with a big love heart on his chest will blah blah blah. You know, like those Jesus statues you see with their hearts all, like, bulging? That's where his powers come from. His magic heart. And it's his powers that get you to stay pure. Without any powers he'd just be a guy telling you not to shag folk and who'd listen to a guy saying that. See when he rips open his shirt and sings "This is who I really am! This is what I'm supposed to do!" you'll totally get the chills so you will. I mean it. You will.

CHUBB: I know I will. I'm getting chills now. So's Fawziya look. Can I also ask…?

DAWN: *(Sings, overlapping.)* "This is who I really am! This is what I'm supposed to do! I'm a beautiful star in his beautiful plan! I am beautiful and so are you!".

DAWN punches her chest twice and points at OZZY, like a tearful athlete dedicating their win. And then she's gone.

There's a pause as the others recover from Hurricane DAWN.

CHUBB notices OZZY is still frozen to the spot, arms full of Miracle Man leaflets, miles away...

CHUBB: Oh aye. I know what you're thinking. You're thinking: "I must, nay, I shall, have that virginity ring off of her finger".

It takes a few beats for this statement to snap OZZY out of his stunned state.

OZZY: No! I'm not thinking that. Jesus Christ, of course I'm not thinking that. *(Beat.)* How, is that what you're thinking?

CHUBB: I've got a feeling I'm off and running on the old quest front that's all. It doesn't hurt that there's a ring involved. Wipe that grin off of Horny Connelly's Hobbitloving coupon. This'll be the real deal...a ring quest rooted in reality. Like when Ponce de Leon was hunting for the Fountain of Youth in South America and he found a ring, bunged it on and suddenly he was turning younger and younger and younger and they could only stop it by cutting off his finger. But it was too late – he was back to being a baby by then. Nightmare. I'd hate to lose a finger. Ponce. There's a name with a bit of fate attached to it eh? No need to ask whether a guy called Ponce was successful in his quests. I tell you man, I think this is all a clue towards my fate. And if you see a clue, you've got to move towards it. See you later Ozzy.

CHUBB exits. OZZY watches him go, miles away.

He has completely forgotten that FAWZIYA is still there.

He looks again at the flyers and shakes his head. Shuts his eyes. What the hell has he agreed to now? After a few moments…

OZZY: *(To himself.)* Make it there's this guy who always does what he's told to do. Until one day he finds a heart: growing, right in the middle of his chest. And it turns him into…a…hero. No. *(Punches his chest, hard.)* Fuck!

He spins round, about to smash something up when he sees FAWZIYA. He freezes. Both are mortified.

Big pause.

To break the ice FAWZIYA produces a huge bag of crisps from her bag.

He really shouldn't but…yes, OZZY will take some. He turns the flip chart round to save it from the shame. He sits beside FAWZIYA and they share the crisps.

It's a wee bit awkward at first but soon they both get lost in thought.

OZZY: We're not hiding.

FAWZIYA: I didn't say we were hiding.

OZZY: No, that's what I'm saying, we're not hiding.

They have some more crisps, psyching themselves up for what they're about to do.

***

FAWZIYA and DAWN are in Dawn's bedroom. Fawziya provides quite a contrast in this world of pink. Miracle Man leaflets are everywhere.

DAWN: The way I see it, this is a war. On one side there's me. Us. The goodies. Fighting for purity and religion and rings and that. And on the other side, there's Fiona Grant. And part of me is like that, this is actually a sin cos she's gonna get totally wiped out know what I mean. Which is sad, cos me and her have been best pals since nursery. And now look. War. But that's what happens. Spreading lies in registration. I've never done half the things she says I've done. First I'm a Timid then I'm a Slag? Slag! No danger. I was too drunk to do anything that night, so she's way off. And all to get in with Hutchy and that. Sad so it is. But I'm totally glad to be out of all that man. The gossip and the bitching and the parties and the good laughs. You're lucky to never have had any pals Fawziya so you are, cos see when they turn against you, it's literally the worst thing in the world. I was like that, Oh my God I'm going to die from like, loneliness or something, you know what I mean? Ha ha ha ha ha! And then, The Miracle Man changed my life. I've had some good ideas in the past I tell you: but this is a…well…a miracle. To switch it round! To turn everyone against her! Everyone in school wearing the rings and totally looking down at her. See me, I can whip up a crowd. I steer public opinion so I do. Just watch. No way could she wear one of those rings. She won't even want to at first. But I'll make sure they're the coolest thing going and not just for the losers. No offence. No-one will see this coming man. I'll be like…we'll both be like…I dunno.

FAWZIYA: Prophets.

DAWN: Puppets?

FAWZIYA: Prophets.

Pause.

DAWN: Puppets?

FAWZIYA: Prophets!

DAWN: Oh prophets. See sometimes Fawziya, you muffle your words so you do. You're like that…"mmmf I'm a, like hhhhhhm".

FAWZIYA: Sorry.

DAWN: No, it's fine but soon you'll be spreading the word so you'll need to be crystal. *(In loud RP.)* "Virginity Rings are ace!" Cos folk need to know that it's not just for Christians or Healy'll veto it. So you're ultra important. Plus it makes it cooler I think. Christianity is the least cool religion, even though it's the best. Well, most famous I mean. How come you don't hang about with the other Asian girls? Rita and that?

FAWZIYA: I don't know. They're a bit…

DAWN: Rita's cool. Hey, you know her brother? He's twenty one and totally in love with me. He writes me notes written in his own blood, says he's going cut his hand off to rid himself of physical temptation. He's lovely. He says it's only his religion that stops him from being with me forever.

FAWZIYA: Well. That, and the law.

DAWN: Aye. I'm totally into religion now. Not like you or Rita's brother. I'm not fundamental. I wasn't brought up to do it I mean. I'm choosing it. Bits of it. Cos see as soon I heard the beat of his opening song: boom boom boom…I was like that, Oh my actual God, this could totally happen. This could be my new thing. And the Miracle Man is hot.

FAWZIYA: Is he?

DAWN: Oh yeah. It wouldn't work if he wasn't I don't think. Cos if a good looking person is saying it's cool to be a virgin then that's different from an ugly person saying it. Know what I mean?

FAWZIYA: Yeah. Em…I wasn't brought up to be religious though. I changed too. Same as you.

DAWN: What, you don't have to wear your…the…?

FAWZIYA: Jilbab. No. It's my choice. So I know…exactly… how you feel. We're very similar. I think.

Pause. DAWN's trying her best to disguise the fact that she can't see too many similarities...

FAWZIYA: *(Cont.)* Em...yeah. Totally. You don't die from loneliness. You just, nearly die. Don't you? And then suddenly there's God, and you're welcomed in and you've got somewhere to go and something to...do. Well, you feel better don't you?

DAWN: Yeah.

FAWZIYA: Yeah. And your mother's wonderful too. Making us tea and crying about human rights in Palestine. That wouldn't happen in my house. My mother hates me. Says she worked all her life to give me a choice and all I do is wind the clock back 200 years. She keeps buying me jeans and leaving them on the bed with little notes in the pockets slagging dad off. I'm probably going to Pakistan to live with my dad when I leave school.

DAWN: Are you? What does he do?

FAWZIYA: He's a prophet. He used to be a solicitor, but then he gave it up to walk from Prestwick to Islamabad. He made a grand gesture, and grand gestures change the world no matter what mum says. He made his choice and took action. And this is my choice. I don't care if he hears about it or not. Cos if everyone was like us, and was just who they were meant to be without trying to be someone older and cool, then no-one would feel so...so sad in the first place. Would they? They would just be who they're meant to be. And that's what The Miracle Man is going to do. Maybe. Do you think?

DAWN: Yeah! God, you should totally make a speech Fawziya.

FAWZIYA: Oh no. No Dawn. I mean...I...I...I...I

DAWN: "I...I...I..." *(Laughing.)* Chill Fawziya. I was only joking. Obviously, I'll do the speech. But if I was off you'd be ace. You're amazing when you don't mumble. We're such a great team. You're the brains and I'm the face. Together we're like a…head. Do you want to do The Pledge To Ourselves?

FAWZIYA: What is it?

DAWN: It's the start of The Pathway. It's a skoosh, relax.

FAWZIYA: I'm sorry. I'm ready.

DAWN: Right, say…I am beautiful.

FAWZIYA: You are beautiful.

DAWN: *(Laughs.)* No! Repeat it!

FAWZIYA: Oh. Sorry. I'm a bit…

DAWN: "I am beautiful".

FAWZIYA: I am…But I'm not.

DAWN: Aye you are.

FAWZIYA: I'm not. I'm fat.

DAWN: It's about what's underneath though.

FAWZIYA: I'm fatter underneath. Even my name is fat. Both of them.

DAWN: Naw. You're made in God's image right. Think about it, there's no way he's up in Heaven looking in a mirror, holding his belly going "Oh man I'm such a fat pig, sure I am Jesus?" *(They laugh.)* Look…

DAWN moves FAWZIYA infront of the mirror.

DAWN: See the thing is…this…Jilbab…it's totally unflattering. No wonder you're a downer on yourself.

FAWZIYA: Well it's supposed to…

DAWN: See.

DAWN has pulled the cloth tighter around FAWZIYA from behind. She moves her hands over FAWZIYA's hips.

DAWN: That's sexy man. I'd fall through the floor for a figure like this I'm telling you. Is this all you can wear? Isn't there anything that could give you a bit more oomph when you check yourself out?

FAWZIYA: I…I suppose I could…Shalwar Kameez might…

DAWN: Just so you feel good about yourself Fawziya know what I mean? If you love yourself you won't just chuck it away with some dobber who doesn't even like you. *(Beat.)* You're a good person aren't you Fawziya?

FAWZIYA: I try to be.

DAWN: You make me feel good. Do you like me?

FAWZIYA: Yes.

DAWN: Really though? Not just…I dunno. Like real friends.

FAWZIYA: Yeah. Real friends.

DAWN: I don't think a boy's going to split us up are they?

FAWZIYA: To be honest, I doubt it.

DAWN smiles. FAWZIYA is looking in the mirror, lost in thought. After a few moments…

FAWZIYA: I think it's time for grand gestures. Action. That's what The Miracle Man would want.

DAWN: Totally.

FAWZIYA: Because it's important. Isn't it? It's good. And it's right.

DAWN: And I'm telling you, everyone will want in on it.

FAWZIYA: *(Smiling, despite herself.)* Will they?

DAWN: Everyone.

***

The next day. The bell rings. OZZY stands awkwardly in Mr HEALY's office like a naughty schoolboy. Mr HEALY is behind his desk leaning back on his chair. He has a kind of wired energy. Too much coffee maybe.

HEALY: Nah, I'm not touching this with a fucking barge pole. It's not that I don't appreciate the gumption – the gumption I like, the idea though, no, something about it worries me. I don't know what exactly, but in a minute I'll be saying "oh that's what's bugging me about this whole shebang" and that'll be that. There's no Techy teachers behind this is there? You've not been approached in the corridor by a shadowy Techy dissident? Because that would be my worry with you – you're susceptible. To coercion. From Techies.

OZZY: No, it all came from a group of fifth years. Apparently it's all the rage.

HEALY: Aye but yo-yos were all the rage and where are they now? Remember when yo-yos were all the rage?

OZZY: Not really.

HEALY: Exactly, I banned them. It was a blink-and-you-miss-it affair. You blinked. So there's no Techy teachers involved? That's something I suppose. Mind you, it's not their M.O. They're too busy plotting my downfall in their sawdust lair to organise assemblies. I swear to Christ Ozzy, on my gravestone you can carve the words "Techy Teachers Did This To Me" cos that's what's going to happen. God they're so paranoid. Noticed that? It's draining, it really is. Psychopaths. Oh aye...how's your dad by the way?

OZZY: Em...fine.

HEALY: Good. Good. Papers weren't too optimistic.

OZZY: Well...ups and downs.

HEALY: I remember when you got the job I was kind of hoping you'd get him along, you know. Talks to the English department, autographed first editions, maybe me and him would have a pub lunch. Introductions could have been made. That didn't happen did it?

OZZY: No.

HEALY: Shame. He's a great man isn't he?

OZZY: Yeah.

HEALY: One of Scotland's truly great men. Apart from the old…

OZZY: Yeah.

HEALY: Must be hard that. Forever in his shadow. Forced to don the tracksuit and piss away your life in the lower leagues with the rest of us also-rans. I can see why you wouldn't even try to compete with him though. It would make it worse, probably. I dread making things worse. When I go, all I ask is that folk say "Well, he didn't make it worse". So it's understandable that you're the way you are is what I'm saying. Here, I remember once he was on Scotland Speaks, you know, that programme. And he was asked about his relationship to Scotland. And he says "I have a sexual relationship with Scotland". Honest. "I have a sexual relationship with Scotland. After a win at Hampden or doing a line of Burns it can get really steamy between Scotland and me. But it's a one night stand. The next day I'm ashamed that I fell for something so cheap, so I bad-mouth her all over town. But I can't keep away. She's an old flame. And she's loose!" Eh? I've always remembered that. It sounds like something I'd say, doesn't it?

Pause.

OZZY: And the thing is Mr Healy, getting back to The Miracle Man, the message is an extremely strong one. And I'm told it's a spectacular show with Hip Hop and Rhythm and Blues and there's an abyss, or something…and the kids all seem to love the fact that each of them gets an engraved…

HEALY: Is it something to do with the religion? Could that be what's bugging me?

OZZY: Oh apparently he doesn't mention Christianity once. It's part of their agreement with the American Government. In fact young Fawziya is very much involved and she's a…well, for want of a better word, Muslim.

HEALY: Yeah I mean, I go to church. I admit it. I have to. Sitting there with all the other living dead, silent for the most part, trying not to fidget or fart, and I encourage that in the school I really do. But the boring stuff, get me? Hard seats, never-ending dirges, dandruffy old duffers talking about fellowship and saying nothing important about nothing. You know where you are with that crap. This… American razzamatazz, has the air of something that might come back and give me a dirty big kick in the arse.

OZZY: Oh no. I don't think that'll happen. If anything it'll be a clean kick. It'll be clean I mean. A nice clean…arse. I don't know what I'm saying really with all this arse stuff. Sorry.

HEALY: *(Choosing to ignore that.)* And okay it's glamorous. I can see that that would be a bonus. It wouldn't be like those shite religious groups we normally have in: acoustic guitars and free cassettes. I'll bet you this Miracle Man guy wouldn't even know what a cassette is!

OZZY: Well, I think he'll know what a cassette is, my point is really that…

HEALY: And he'll have a great big bus eh? Not a crappy wee transit van like those losers trundle up in. His bus'll have TVs, fridges, beds, the works. I'll bet it goes "hhhsssss" when it stops. I'd love that. I swear to God I would love a bus like that. Try undermining me when I roll up in the playground in one of those beasts. Just try it! "DOOOOOO! Move it ya dirty, techy, tie-tucked-in bastards!". And any hassle from the senior management team about that Investors In People fiasco and that would be it: I'd hit the highway, never come back. *(Singing.)* "East bound and down, loaded up and trucking, we're gonna do what they said can't be done…"

OZZY: Mr Healy…

HEALY: "…we got a long way to go, and a short time to get there, I'm east bound just to watch old bandit run"

OZZY: Mr Healy…

HEALY: Smoky and The Bandit. Classic.

OZZY: Yeah. So. Does that mean that we can get the ball rolling with the invitation? Apparently there's a deadline.

HEALY: *(Conspiratorially.)* And here…think of the action you'd get with a bus like that. I'll bet you this Miracle Man's beating them off with a stick eh?

OZZY: Well I doubt it. It's a virginity pledge remember. He's a virgin. They all are.

HEALY: Aaaah! That's it! That's what's bugging me about this whole shebang! Virginity. Why don't they want to lose their virginity?

OZZY: Oh em…teen pregnancy, STDs, self-esteem. *(Reading from a leaflet.)* "You could argue that the same sex campaign has failed…"

HEALY: No, no, no. I know why we don't want them to lose their virginity. But why don't they want to do it? How come the kids are buying this? Are there famous folk signed up to it or something? Is that it? Does this Miracle Man have Hollywood connections?

OZZY: Em…probably, I don't really…probably.

Pause.

HEALY: Introductions may be made. Is that what you're saying?

OZZY: I'm sure that would be no problem. He'd be happy to introduce you to…somebody. Probably. Maybe. And as for the kids, I think to be honest a lot of them just like his music. And the rings are a nice touch.

HEALY: Rings?

OZZY: Oh yeah they love the rings. They all get a ring when they pledge to stay pure till marriage.

HEALY: Bzzzz!! Vetoed! Red card! Next!

OZZY: What?

HEALY: Rings. Final straw. No rings. No jewellery. Not on my watch. The dream is over son.

OZZY: But that's the…

HEALY: You should've mentioned the rings at the get go Ozzy, saved yourself a lunch hour.

OZZY: Well most of these evangelical virginity things have rings, I assumed you'd…

HEALY: "No rings. No jewellery. No white trainers or football colours. Smart black trousers or skirts. Ties."

OZZY: It's religious though doesn't that make a difference?

HEALY: Thought you said it wasn't religious?

OZZY: Well it's kind of religious.

HEALY: No. Keep coming with the suggestions though. Separates you from the you know whos.

OZZY: But…but maybe he…he can…

HEALY: What? He can what?

OZZY: He… *(Pause.)* No. No, you're right, it's daft. Sorry. Long shot. Don't know how I got talked into it really. Sorry.

HEALY: No harm done. At least I know your interests now – I'm getting a wee sense of who you really are at last. For future reference. You're a Holy Joe who's passionate about virgins. *(Points to his head.)* That's replaced the previous file, know what I mean?

OZZY: Well I'm not really…

HEALY: *(Conspiratorially again.)* Funny story. First time I ever had sex it was on a see-saw with a girl who'd just been fired from Woolworths. Horrible experience. Sick making. A truly horrible experience for all concerned. Like em…well, it was similar to what I imagine Vietnam must've been like. Anyway, after the whole sorry façade had ground to a halt, she says to me…and this is my point…she said to me, "your brother was better". Imagine that? That's haunted me that. So…I feel your pain. But you've got to get back on that see saw. Hear me Ozzy? It's the only way. Get back on the see saw. And don't worry about the kids. I'll bet you a fiver they've already forgotten all about it. Trust me, it's a blink and you'll miss it yo-yo throwback. It's already over.

***

Eh…Nope. The school is absolutely buzzing with it. Posters appear everywhere and flyers are handed out to the crowds at break.

A banner reads, "The Miracle Man is coming, sign up NOW!!!"

DAWN and FAWZIYA are doing the cheer-leading. Well, DAWN is. FAWZIYA is hanging back. FAWZIYA is wearing her Shalwar Kameez (trousers and a tunic.).

She seems to be extremely uncomfortable, hiding behind DAWN as she passionately spreads the word. But DAWN soon notices her new pal is dodging the limelight and drags her to the front and begins to instruct her on how to hold the crowd's attention. It's all in the pose, apparently: hips out, fish pout, Miss America totter and Oscar-loser's laugh.

FAWZIYA finds this all deeply embarrassing at first and struggles hellishly to follow DAWN's lead. But very soon the whole escapade strikes her as just bloody ridiculous. The only sensible option left is to take the piss.

So, suddenly she launches into an exaggerated pastiche of DAWN's moves, mimicking her gushing machine gun speech too, as she falls over herself to attract the crowd's attention.

Then she stops, wondering if she took that too far.

After thinking for a beat, DAWN laughs. A real laugh. FAWZIYA's right – that does look ridiculous. Both girls are laughing now and happily go back to handing out the flyers, this time shoulder to shoulder.

Somehow, FAWZIYA's joke has made it easier for her to be the focus of the playground's attention and in DAWN's company. And DAWN's a wee bit different too – more restrained, more natural.

It feels good.

They're enjoying this.

The crowd builds – more and more leaflets, louder and louder, chanting and cheering.

The Miracle Man is coming!

***

In LEWIS' hospital room. There are no machines, no flickering stars here now. Just a bed and a chair and the usual flowers, water jugs etc.

LEWIS lies still on the bed, eyes closed, as OZZY paces about, in the middle of a story...

OZZY: So the guy decides to kill himself. That way, as well as dodging the illness, he'll be doing something – taking action. Finally. Making a grand gesture that even his brother could never match.

But this guy's a coward isn't he? He wouldn't do it. It wouldn't happen. He'll never do anything so how...?

No, right, okay. He would do it, but he has to force himself. He has to make it happen. He ties himself to a chair in front of the oven. Fastens himself down – knots tightened with his teeth. He gives himself no choice.

And…and, yeah. Before he ties himself down he gets the TV set up, right by the oven. He wants to be found watching an old tape of his dad doing an interview. It'll add intrigue he reckons. Maybe it'll make it look like they were closer than they actually were? Maybe it'll connect them at last, in death if not in life. He clicks on the remote control and chucks it across the room. He tightens the last knot.

The door opens and PAULA comes in holding clean sheets and a change of clothes for LEWIS. She's about speak when she realises what's going on. She sits down silently and OZZY ploughs on. He has his back to her and hasn't seen her…

So there he is, tied down and drunk on the gas that's filling the room, watching his old boy witter on about having a sexual relationship with Scotland or something when suddenly…em…yeah, the tape rolls and his dad's corrugated, whiskey-battered face is replaced by…Jamie Oliver.

Jamie Oliver? Jamie Bloody Oliver! Talking about school diners and fat kids dying from Monster Munch. He cannae believe it! He taped over his "Dad" tape!

Then it hits him. Shit. He's going to be found dead, tied to a kitchen chair, watching a Jamie Oliver video! As a final gesture that makes very little sense. Where's the mystery now? Where's the drama?

But the remote control is on the other side of the room. Got to get to it before the gas takes hold! He tries to bump his chair over. Bump, scrape, breath, bump, scrape SHIT arrgh!

The chair topples and he falls face down, hard onto the kitchen floor, hands and feet still bound fast.

"This", thinks the guy, "is fucking typical".

Then just as he thinks it's all over…from out of nowhere… suddenly…

Em…Suddenly…

OZZY is struggling to come up with something so turns to pace the room but sees, for the first time, PAULA sitting there smiling.

He freezes.

He looks back to his father and then again to PAULA. PAULA smiles again. She indicates "go on".

He sits down.

PAULA: Suddenly…?

He shakes his head.

PAULA: Come on.

OZZY: Nah.

PAULA: I told you, talking's good. Sometimes you can see people really flinch when you say something like "I love you".

OZZY: Yeah. Yeah, I've noticed that.

PAULA: People in comas I mean.

OZZY: *(Slightly offended.)* I know.

PAULA: Stories are a good idea. I'd love someone to tell me stories.

OZZY: It's just something I do to…you know.

PAULA: I know but it's good. You're good. Aw please?

OZZY: Nah. It's a neck.

PAULA: How is it? It's just me and I know hee haw about stories. Here, guess how long it's been since I've read a good book? Three years. Three years and not a single good story. Trouble is, every book I read's got a guy wearing a

balaclava on the cover. They were the only books my ex
would have in the house – balaclava books. My bookcase
is a balaclava-rama: SAS, Hardmen, Explorers and they're
all duff. They should ban balaclavas shouldn't they? I
mean, who's buying a balaclava for legitimate purposes
these days? Just to wear down the shops when it's a bit
nippy? No-one. Show me a man who owns a balaclava
and I'll show you a suspect. *(No response from her audience.)*
So anyway, I'm gagging for stories and I've nothing to
compare it too so it's win win really. No, tell a lie, when
Lewis first came in I got *Thomas The Rhymer* out of the
library. I was trying to turn a new page, I think, but no joy.
I got stuck in the prologue.

OZZY: Yeah it's quite…challenging.

PAULA: *(At the same time.)* Boring. I know. It seems like it's
mostly him going on about how there always has to be
two sides fighting against each other before anything good
happens. And a lot about god as well. He really hates
god doesn't he? Or am I getting that wrong? I was quite
confused. And sleepy.

OZZY: No that's him. Actually when my mum left, at the
bottom of the note she wrote that she was going to start the
search for Fingal in Lourdes. Just to wind him up I think.

PAULA: Did it work?

OZZY: He didn't smile again.

PAULA: And is she in Lourdes right enough?

OZZY: God knows.

PAULA: Well. Sorry Lewis pet, you're too clever for me.
I'll stick with it though. It would be nice to say I'd read
something like *Thomas The Rhymer.* I could learn bits of it to
quote when I want to dispense wisdom. You can't do that
so much with balaclava books. Hey, maybe if there was a
balaclava in it things would improve?

OZZY: In *Thomas The Rhymer*? Don't hold your breath.

PAULA: No, in your story. You should put a balaclava in it and see what happens.

OZZY: "And suddenly…he's wearing a balaclava"?

PAULA: No. And suddenly there's a knock at the door. He… what's his name by the way? Can't keep calling him, the "guy"?

OZZY: He doesn't have a name.

PAULA: Just tell me.

OZZY: Well. Fingal. In my head, his name is Fingal. It's nothing to do with my brother though. I mean I don't really know anything about…

PAULA: Right, Fingal's on the floor, tied to his chair and the knocks keep coming. And he's like that "go away!" But a voice from behind the door says…

OZZY: A woman's voice.

PAULA: Aye, a woman's voice says…em…

OZZY: "Are you killing yourself in there by any chance pet?"

PAULA: Ha! Yeah. "No!" says Fingal.

OZZY: "Well I think you are".

PAULA: "Who are you? I mean go away!"

OZZY: "They've changed the gas you know. You can't gas yourself with modern oven gas". Changed the gas? That sounds about bloody right Fingal thinks. "I'm coming in" she says. "No! The door's locked!" But it's not and in walks a woman wearing a long black coat, black high heels and a jet black…

BOTH: Balaclava.

PAULA: Nice.

OZZY: *(Cont.)* She has an air of calm about her though. She leaves a fresh, kind of, lemonade scent where the gas used to be…

PAULA: It's called Soda. Very expensive. It was a gift and it's nearly finished. Carry on.

OZZY: Fingal thinks that she's the angel of death.

PAULA: Ach no.

OZZY: Well she is wearing a balaclava Paula. It's a logical assumption.

PAULA: Maybe though…no. Right. She unties him. And when she's down, close to him, he gets this…tingling feeling. He knows this woman! But who could it be? Then she goes over to the kitchen work surface and pulls herself up onto it, crossing her legs – and as she does, her coat opens a wee bit and Fingal catches a glimpse. She's naked under there!

OZZY: *(Not convinced.)* Naked?

PAULA: Totally naked. And she says…em…

OZZY: "This is who you really are. You're The Miracle Man. You're going to save the day and be a hero.". And he says "No, I'm not. That's not me. I'm not the one. I'm the fake. I'm the impostor. I can't save anybody. Look at me".

PAULA: And she says "Oh I'm looking alright big boy". And she slowly undoes her coat and…they totally end up shagging.

OZZY: Shagging? No.

PAULA: How not?

OZZY: It's a bit…

PAULA: What? There's total tension. She's right there. In the room. Naked. Underneath. She can keep the balaclava on if that helps.

OZZY: I know but…Nah.

PAULA: What then?

OZZY: Well. Maybe, instead, she…takes out a platinum plated Zippo lighter that has the word "ABYSS" etched on it and sexily lights a cigarette?

PAULA: In a room full of gas?

OZZY: Aye. Exactly.

PAULA: So that's it? It ends in a great big explosion? You'd rather have a great big explosion than shagging?

OZZY: It's not the end. They don't have ends. They're just ideas to get him going. What?

PAULA: Nothing.

OZZY: Why are you in the huff?

PAULA: I'm not.

OZZY: You look like…

PAULA: *(In the huff.)* Well I'm not!

Pause. She can't keep silences…

PAULA: Have you found Fingal? The real Fingal I mean?

OZZY: No.

PAULA: Well maybe…

OZZY: I know.

PAULA: I'm just saying that your dad's on The Pathway now and…

OZZY: I know. Look I do understand Paula. I'm not as thick as everyone thinks.

PAULA: I don't think…

OZZY: Yes you do. And don't give me this PE teachers are dumb-dumbs stuff. Guidance Paula, Guidance. I'm Guidance as well as PE, so I do actually understand information and emotions and…and…pathways. I'm not a bloody child! *(Instant change.)* I'm so sorry. I'm sorry.

PAULA: It's okay.

OZZY: No, I didn't mean to…

PAULA: It's okay. It's just part of it. Everybody snaps.

OZZY: But you've been so good. From day one. I…

PAULA: Ozzy, look at my face. It's okay. I've been doing this for years. Sometimes it's my job to catch the snap it's normal. Everything that happens in this room is normal. Everything.

Pause.

OZZY: *(Shakes his head.)* These stories. That's not normal. Not for me anyway. I think the idea was he'd like one so much he'd want to write about it and…and come to life or something. That's my master plan! That's what I've come up with when left to my own devices and told to talk. Pathetic eh?

PAULA: No.

OZZY: He hasn't written a word for years and I think my bargain basement inspiration will do what medicine can't? Aye right. So you're bang on, it should be Fingal here, or mum, or anyone better – but it's not. It's me. And I can't do it. I can't take the weight man.

Pause.

PAULA: Look…I was thinking of going for a drink tonight. Not a big session or anything, just pour it down me until I get sick, teary and violent. You're welcome to join me if you're good in a fight.

OZZY: No.

PAULA: Oh.

OZZY: No way.

PAULA: Okay.

OZZY: No thanks I mean.

PAULA: Right.

OZZY: I can't.

PAULA: No that's fine. Honestly. Inappropriate. God I really must stop taking the patients' medication, it goes straight to my head sometimes. You've probably got like…

OZZY: Oh no it's not that. It's just…you know…it's a school night.

***

The bell rings. Monday. FAWZIYA and DAWN are sitting eating their very healthy looking lunches. CHUBB stands beside them. DAWN has just grabbed the poster out of his hand. She's raging…

DAWN: A ring ban!?

CHUBB: Anyone caught wearing a ring will be suspended. *(Holding out his left hand, he's wearing a ring.)* I'm teetering on the edge of the law. Just the way I like it. Virginity ring. Well, my dad's wedding ring, same difference.

DAWN: But rings are the whole point of it.

FAWZIYA: Well, they're not the whole point of it.

DAWN: *(Snippy.)* Folk have got to get rings Fawziya.

FAWZIYA: Yeah but that's not the whole point of it.

DAWN: Aw no way man! This is totally racist or something.

CHUBB: Ozzy's been accused of that in the past Dawn. No smoke without fire so sayeth the Lord.

DAWN: Oh my God. If there's no rings the Miracle Man might not even come.

CHUBB: He's not coming. It's unofficial but I have my sources. Loose lips in the office. Healy's said no to the whole thing.

DAWN: What do you mean he said no? How can he not be coming? What happened?

CHUBB: Ozzy must've bottled it. He's a bottler. Member that staff-pupils hockey match where it looked like he was going to cry?

DAWN: It was a dead cert! It was a lock! We've told everyone.

FAWZIYA: Maybe we could speak to Mr Healy ourselves?

DAWN: Ozzy must've sabotaged us. That's the only explanation. He lied to our face and then grassed us up to Healy!

FAWZIYA: Why would he do that?

DAWN: Duh, Fawziya. To score points.

CHUBB: And he could do with the points there's no denying it – Healy hates him.

DAWN: He's screwed us over! I cannot believe this!

FAWZIYA: *(Seriously.)* Neither can I. Look, don't panic Dawn. We can appeal. We can protest. In fact a protest would be amazing actually, cos not only would it steer public opinion, it would adhere to The Miracle Man's teaching. Like, when he was in his gang back in Detroit and they all wanted him to smuggle drugs in his rectum but he didn't want to do it, so just as they were all going through airport security he make the ultimate protest and stripped off all his clothes and pledged himself to God. I was crying at that bit.

DAWN: So was I.

CHUBB: Okay okay. I get it. Say no more. Protests, miracles, rectums. You're pushing my buttons and I've got to tell you, it's nice. I'll do it.

DAWN: Do what?

CHUBB: There are some, when faced with a challenge upon the road towards their ultimate quest, who will wither and turn away. But I am not such a man. I leave you a Knight, who begs only your gentle gaze and an approving wave of your...I dunno, fan, or whatever.

DAWN: Aye okay, very good.

CHUBB is lingering...

CHUBB: *(To FAWZIYA.)* You look different. Not quite so...

DAWN: She looks cool so what?

CHUBB shrugs, does an elaborate bow and runs off.

DAWN: That guy is...

FAWZIYA: Unique.

DAWN: Oh my god.

FAWZIYA: What?

DAWN: I didn't say anything.

FAWZIYA: *(Serious.)* You did. And I don't. I won't. I would never.

DAWN: Whatever.

FAWZIYA: Unique is not necessarily good.

DAWN: Whatever Fawziya, God. I've got more important things to worry about now than you fancying roly poly morons. Grow up.

They eat for a bit, in a silent huff.

A big cheer goes up somewhere off. Then a low "oooh!" from a crowd.

When they hear a massive "whayhey!" coming from the same direction the girls can stand it no longer and run off to see what's going on.

***

CHUBB has somehow got himself onto the roof of the school. It's really not that high but he's clinging to a chimney for dear life and is quaking with terror – still desperately putting on a show for the crowd below.

FAWZIYA and DAWN join the crowd looking up, riveted.

CHUBB: Listen up losers! Witness a miracle! I was once like you. Crippled with…with fear…and absolute, really bad, terror…but I've been cured so I have! The Miracle Man cured me! I once suffered from The Vertigo, as those of you who were standing underneath the umbrellas that time at Butlins will no doubt testify. But now, see, as I glide along the rooftops like…Spiderman or some prick. Look at me gliding! The Miracle Man did this! If I'm like this, think what he could do for a bunch of hellbent buggers like yourselves! But you have been denied the opportunity of salvation and a kick ass assembly by a corrupt and prejudiced system so you have.

HEALY arrives – raging.

HEALY: What the hell is this? Who the hell is that? Hey! Get the hell down from there now you!

CHUBB holds his head and wobbles a bit.

FAWZIYA: He's going to fall.

HEALY: That guttering is not built to hold heavier boned pupils. Get down now or I'll send the Janny up there with carte blanche to nip you in the fireman's hold.

CHUBB: Healy is censoring your freedom to worship, your freedom to have a healthy life, your freedom to wear a cool ring!

HEALY: What's he on about? *(Shouting.)* What you on about?!

CHUBB: Ozzy MacDonald has connived with Mr Healy in a racist plot to make all of our lives a total bummer!

HEALY: Racist…? Jesus God. *(To FAWZIYA.)* Get Mr MacDonald! Go!

FAWZIYA runs off.

CHUBB: So…to complete my protest against this injustice…I will follow in the Miracle Man's footsteps and…and…oh God…strip down to the…to the buff.

DAWN: Gadz! This is a shame.

CHUBB tries to undress whilst clinging on for dear life and not fainting. By the end he's got as far as topless.

CHUBB: Dawn! Dawn is that you?

DAWN: Aw naw.

CHUBB: Dawn West. Let it be known hencewith…I love you! And to complete my quest, will you, in front of Horny Connelly and this crowd of gawking fudds, confirm your love for me?

DAWN: O…M…G. This. Is. A. Pure. Neck!!! *(Shouting.)* I hardly know this guy! I think he's a dick too. Don't let him put you off The Miracle Man! He's a whatdoyoumacallit… an arsehole.

FAWZIYA has returned with OZZY.

CHUBB: I can't hear you! Are you saying that you love me too? Dawn? Is that what your saying? Your expression is obscure.

It's not.

OZZY: Chubb get down from there right this minute!

CHUBB: Dawn! I'm going to have to push you for an answer.

DAWN: You're a dick! Shut up! I don't like you! You're ruining everything!

CHUBB: Oh. Oh. Oh well then. Everything...seems to be... rushing towards me. I think I'm either fainting or...going... into...hyperspace!

FAWZIYA: Robert hang on! Robert!

CHUBB: What? Who...called me...who...?

CHUBB lets go of whatever he's holding onto, puts his hands to his face and swoons into a faint. He falls right off the roof.

OZZY: CHUBB!!!!

OZZY runs towards him. His arms wide.

***

In the hospital waiting room a little later. OZZY sits between FAWZIYA and DAWN. They all look equally fed up.

DAWN: *(To OZZY.)* And to think, he died because of what you did.

OZZY: He's not dead.

DAWN: He could be dead. Because of what you did.

OZZY: He was one floor up. And he didn't hit the ground – I caught him. Something I got no thanks for by the way. It's my back I'm worried about. All over my shoulders and right down across my chest. Agony.

OZZY runs his hands over his chest. His fingers find something he doesn't like. He's preoccupied with that during the rest of the scene...

DAWN: It's always about you Sir, isn't it?

OZZY: Mm?

DAWN: Nothing. Judas.

FAWZIYA: I think what we're saying Sir is that we need to get people together to debate what exactly happened with The Miracle Man Ban as soon as. Not to mention the accusations, or this could all be for nothing.

OZZY: What accusations? *(About his chest.)* Ahya. What the hell is…?

DAWN: There's nothing to debate Fawziya. It was a betrayal. End of. *(To OZZY.)* And I tell you what, I'm going to make it my business to steer public opinion right back round to The Miracle Man so it totally gets the playground buzzing and literally crushes you to death in the process Sir. So I am. No offence.

OZZY: Uh huh.

FAWZIYA: But how though? Everyone's saying it's done and dusted. Even Robert's protest didn't work. Most folk seem to think that was just about you and him hooking up or something.

DAWN: We're not hooking up! Gadz.

FAWZIYA: I know. Do you think you will though? After this I mean?

DAWN: Fawziya, he is a never ending bawbag. Open your eyes.

FAWZIYA: So you're not going to go out with him then? Ever?

DAWN: Open your eyes! I came to the hospital because I'm lovely – that's all. I'm a caring person. But that doesn't mean I care about Chubb. Cos I don't. No-one does. There's a bigger picture here: in a matter of days The Miracle Man packs up his rings and flies for home. We need to come up with something as soon as.

FAWZIYA: Yeah. Well, maybe we should just ask Mr MacDonald what really happened…?

DAWN: *(Overlapping.)* What really happened was he sold us out! Look at him. He lets people down that's what he does. Don't you Sir?

OZZY: *(Miles away, hand down his shirt now.)* Aye.

DAWN: *(To FAWZIYA.)* Are you going to let me down now too Fawziya? Is that it? Now you've got the blusher and the heels and the guys giggling in the corridor? Are you going to forget all about me and The Miracle Man and swan off transformed?

FAWZIYA: I'm not…I want the Miracle Man to come to the school just as much as you do Dawn.

DAWN: Well why don't you think of a way to get the playground buzzing then? Cos I can't do everything. *(Sigh.)* You know Fawziya, in many ways, I'm only human. *(Getting up.)* I'll be in the magazines.

DAWN strops off.

After a moment…

FAWZIYA: I don't think you sold us out Sir. That's not who you are. Is it? Not really.

OZZY stands, distracted to the point of almost not being here.

OZZY: Aye look. Em. I have to…to em…take my shirt off. So. Yeah. You stay here okay? Don't leave these seats I won't be long.

He starts to head off.

FAWZIYA: Sir?

OZZY: What?

FAWZIYA: I believe in you.

OZZY: Why are you saying that?

FAWZIYA: I don't know.

Beat.

OZZY: Just…just stay there okay?

OZZY exits.

PAULA enters from the other direction with CHUBB. CHUBB is wearing a neck brace and a shell-shocked expression.

FAWZIYA: Oh God. Are you okay?

CHUBB: No.

PAULA: He's fine. He doesn't really need the neck brace. He requested it. Where's Mr MacDonald?

FAWZIYA: He said he had to change his shirt or something.

CHUBB: Change his shit probably. Get his shit changed. I know what he means. It's time I made some changes in the shit department too. In every department. I swear to god, when I was falling there, through the abyss, I saw my future. And it's a lonely, lonely thing. Is that how it's to be? Laughed at, lonely and falling? Look at me Fawziya – heart broken, reputation in tatters, possibly suspended, neck problems…

PAULA: You don't have neck problems.

CHUBB: No, this is a turning point for me. I'm toeing the establishment line from now on. I'm going straight to Healy's office to help clear up this mess and save my name. I'll beg if I have to. I can't fall any further.

PAULA: Ach that's a shame. There are some who would say that a another serious fall might do you some good.

CHUBB: Pfft! I know. Horny Connelly for one. Sent me a text there saying I'm out of Lolq. He says the V Team is directly opposed to the free-love tenets of the Legion and I've made my bed so I can wank in it. So much for my only friend eh? I've got to make some changes man or it's the abyss for me.

FAWZIYA: But we're not opposed to anyone. Why can't people see that The Miracle Man is all about bringing people together for the good, not splitting them up?

PAULA: Because it's unnatural pet. That's not how good stuff happens. Sorry. None of my business but, you know, it goes against nature, what you just said there.

CHUBB and FAWZIYA exchange a confused look. PAULA feels the need to elaborate…

PAULA: The natural state of the world is revolution. The only way for good to prevail is to understand that life is war, with at least two forces opposed against each other, day in day out. "It's a fight whose only synthesis is not an end at all – not destruction, but the beginning of yet another fight". Long story short, two sides at war will get results, so don't sweat it. *(Beat.)* That was me dispensing wisdom by the way. Feeeeels goooooood.

PAULA points off, asking if that's where OZZY went. FAWZIYA nods. PAULA exits, delighted at her wisdom dispensing skills.

CHUBB: She fancies me I think. But god knows I'm done with women.

FAWZIYA: *(Lightbulb.)* We need to find Dawn.

CHUBB: How?

FAWZIYA: I'll tell you when we get Dawn.

CHUBB: It's not Eastenders Fawziya. The episode won't end when you tell me your idea.

FAWZIYA: I just want to get us all together to talk about it, what's so wrong with that?

CHUBB: I can't. No more trouble. No more rebelling for me.

FAWZIYA: Oh Robert c'mon.

CHUBB: No, I can't. You didn't see what I saw. There's stars down there, but nothing else. I can't.

FAWZIYA rolls her eyes and then starts to head off...

CHUBB: Hey. I heard you on the roof by the way. Calling me Robert now eh?

FAWZIYA: That's your name isn't it? *(Turning.)* Is that why you fainted?

CHUBB: No. Unrelated vertigo incident. How? Do you want that to be the reason I fainted?

FAWZIYA: I don't know. Do you want that I would want that to be the reason you fainted?

CHUBB: Depends if you want that I want that you want...

FAWZIYA: *(Interrupting.)* To be honest I really need to...

CHUBB: No fair enough. Catch you later.

She's gone.

CHUBB: I hope.

CHUBB's on his own.

***

In LEWIS' darkened hospital room. He lies still, silent and dying, as before. OZZY has his shirt off and his back to us, standing close to a mirror, examining his chest.

PAULA comes in, lighting the room from outside as she slowly opens the door. OZZY turns to face her, like a child.

In the centre of his chest is a large, smooth lump – shaped like a loveheart.

Just as OZZY is about to speak, LEWIS gasps. His eyes are still shut but the breath is powerful, hard and sharp.

LEWIS is coming to life.

End of Part One

Part Two

In LEWIS' hospital room. Things have changed here again. This time, by the looks of it, for the better.

LEWIS is hooked up to machines as when we first saw him, but he's more upright, has more colour, displays the odd bit of movement. In short, he looks better.

And just for the moment there's the feeling of a new day with OZZY too. He's laughing and has, for the duration of PAULA's story, forgotten all about the dreaded heart.

PAULA's laughing too – wiping her eyes. She has her coat on over her uniform and looks comfortable in the room, like she's been here for a while. They're laughing throughout this...

OZZY: Oh my god it's disgusting! What did you do?

PAULA: What could I do? I tapped him on the shoulder and said "excuse me I think you might've had a wee accident". But he'd been sleeping for a good ten minutes by then so I couldn't wake him.

OZZY: And was it all...?

PAULA: No, he was wearing a Johnny so it had gone skooshing out down-the-way. Ruined my mum's couch though. You can only turn cushions over so many times. And he was heavy as well so I couldn't even move him. I had to lie there, in it, till he got cramp in his fingers and woke up.

OZZY: It's so romantic.

PAULA: Well see up till then, it actually was quite romantic. It was just nerves. And Strawberry Wine. And he was very apologetic when he woke up.

OZZY: I should bloody think so.

PAULA: The first time doesn't matter anyway. It's never perfect. It's all the other times that count.

OZZY: Did you ever hear what happened to the guy?

PAULA: I know what happened to him. I married him.

OZZY: You married him? The guy falls asleep on you, half way through your very first time, rolls over, wets himself, and you think "this one's a keeper!".

PAULA: I come from a small town, there's a desert island mentality. And when he was young JJ was hilarious. He'd tell you these great big wonderful stories about all the messes he'd get into and you'd be on the edge of your seat so you would. Mind you I wasn't laughing when it was me left to clean up the messes while he was off keeping another girl on the edge of her much younger, slighter slimmer seat. But hey ho I'm not bitter. Right you. Loosing your virginity. Let's go.

OZZY: Ach mine isn't as funny as that.

PAULA: I'll bet you a fiver it's quite funny. All virginity stories are quite funny.

OZZY: Nah. It was just…as you would expect.

PAULA gets up and takes some chocolates from a box beside Lewis' bed.

PAULA: Come on Ozzy. Tell me a story. Please.

OZZY: Well. Okay. Right, well, when I lost my virginity, I was dressed as a strongman. That's quite funny isn't it?

PAULA: You were dressed as a strongman?

OZZY: Yeah.

PAULA: You were quite a confused teenager weren't you?

OZZY: Yeah. Yeah I was.

OZZY chuckles a bit and there's a pause. As far as he's concerned that's the end of the anecdote. Paula has other ideas…

PAULA: And?

OZZY: And what?

PAULA: "And what?" And all the other stuff. The story. The rest of it. C'mon. Spill.

OZZY stands up and shuts his eyes for a minute. Deep breath. When he opens them he's different.

OZZY: Make it there's this guy. A young guy. A confused teenager, stuck in a damp and hungover mansion with his mad mother and his famous dad. And it all meant nothing in particular until one Easter weekend, when his parents were away hitting the skids and causing chaos, his brother came home.

His brother was only a few years older but he'd lived a million lives even by then. Kicked out of Uni after Uni; year-long vanishing acts; drug busts; celebrity pregnancy scares you name it. And here he was. In the flesh. Strolling up the gravel drive with a troupe of disciples like something from an art film.

There were magicians, strippers, transvestites, old guys with mandolins and two car loads of university girls, all of whom were drinking Cider from a jug, which the guy took to be a sign of great sophistication. And still does as it goes.

The brother announced that he was back to have a "Resurrection Party". Good Friday everything would be death: Halloween costumes, heavy metal; Saturday would be a John and Yoko style Bed-In; and Sunday... Resurrection: a rave. The brother took the guy to the side and told him he was to have a special role in this shindig. The younger brother, the confused teen, was to help them tip over a big garden sculpture that was in orchard; push it down the hill and into the river. It was to be like the rock in front of Jesus's cave. Massive big ugly thing it was, like a cross between his father's face and a fist. Everybody hated it. The older brother called it the Bogging Boulder. That part of the weekend was to be called the Last Hurrah, and when it was done they could finally live. How wrong he was.

But the guy had a job! Push over the sculpture! They even had a costume for him. A strongman suit. And the guy was...so...proud. That his brother wanted him – no – *needed* him. Thought of him.

But god he was nervous. He didn't really join in with the rest of party, just sat at the top of the stairs listening.

Till late on Sunday night, close to his big moment and in full costume, he hears a knock at his bedroom door. A girl. Off her nut and madly in love with his father, she says she wants to watch a video of the great man on *Scotland Speaks*. Could she watch it here? Everyone was talking about the programme cos he'd been drunk and insulted loads of people. So they put it on. They kissed. They had sex. It was his first time.

Beat.

And right then...right, right at that moment...the story starts. The story everyone knows. That you know. Probably. The story of the rest of his life.

See, he didn't go to roll the sculpture down the hill. He was "preoccupied". But everyone else did. All of them drunk and high and messing about. Well somehow they tipped the bloody thing over and it was on a massive circular steel plinth and it just sped off down the slope, slipped from their grip...

And someone got trapped. Caught. Pulled under. His name was Tom Gowrie. A student – a guy who'd only met Fingal – met the older brother – a week before. Fate. He was pulled into the river. And he was dead when they dragged him out.

By the time the guy, the confused, recently de-flowered guy, heard the commotion and made it down there, the brother had gone. Fled. Forever.

The mother smashed up a whole room with the police watching. She went on TV with blood on her face. She said she was going to look for her son and bring him home to prove his innocence, but no-one believed that really. She was just gone.

Then the Dad, the famous dad with his genius for words, made some gag about how the real tragedy was that Fingal had taken the Jag and that got in the papers and…it was a siege after that.

Then came the interview. The mother's Tell-All. The guy handed the paper to his father expecting him to deny it. Fool that he was. But instead the father scanned the headline and slammed the office door. They've spoken maybe ten times since.

And what did she say? What was the controversy? Can't you remember? Well, it was a smear job, to save herself. She said that the father was a fake. Not only had he not written a word of the tome which had made his name around the globe – she had done that – but he was also a fake father. One of her boys belonged to the great man, while the other one…didn't.

Oh don't worry, this is no mystery story. It's right here for everyone to see. They're clever and he is…he was…I was… strong.

Strong. But I didn't hold the sculpture. And I didn't save anyone.

And here I am.

For everyone to see. At the end.

OZZY runs his hands over his shoulders and onto his chest.

PAULA: God Ozzy. God pet. It's no wonder you're…

OZZY: What?

PAULA: Broken hearted I was going to say. It's no wonder you have a broken heart.

OZZY: I don't. Is that…is that what you think? No I'm not that. No. I'm…fine with it actually. I'm just like everyone else Paula. Except of course that I have a cancerous heart growing in the centre of my chest. But hey ho I'm not bitter.

PAULA: You don't know that's what it is. No-one does until the tests come back. There's no point imagining the worst. It could be anything, clogged pores, an allergy…

OZZY: An allergy?

PAULA: And before you say it, the lumps and bumps that Lewis has are secondary developments on his bones from his prostate cancer. These things happen in chronological order and they aren't hereditary.

OZZY: Well. That doesn't matter. He's not my real dad.

PAULA: And anyway, I don't think it looks that much like a heart.

OZZY: Oh it's a heart. Had to be a heart.

PAULA: There's a medical explanation for everything.

OZZY: Is there a medical explanation for this? *(Lewis.)* I was told he had hours left and now look.

PAULA: Well this is…unusual. But as I said, a sudden upturn can be as much a warning sign as a sudden…

OZZY: Could it've been the stories? Did that work do you think?

PAULA: I don't really…it's…maybe.

OZZY: Doesn't matter. Doesn't matter.

Pause.

PAULA: The other day I was talking to a doctor in the corridor about an old woman who had just passed away. I said the cause of death should be loneliness. The doctor said that no matter what it feels like, loneliness doesn't kill you. I thought that was a comfort. Of sorts. But then when I was in my bed that night I thought, no, she's wrong. Loneliness does kill you. It just doesn't kill you immediately.

OZZY: Are you saying that you're broken hearted?

PAULA: No. I'm saying I'm just like everyone else.

***

There's a buzzing noise…

It's a live microphone. DAWN appears in a spotlight and tentatively (for her) speaks…

DAWN: Well…em…We're like that, how come the school lets Asian pupils wear Jilbabs and Shalwar Kameez, that are total Health and Safety risks and banned from every school in France, but when it comes to a tiny wee ring, a ring that protects my purity, a ring that's a sign of my faith, my Christianity, it gets banned? There's two rules so there is, one for them and one for us. Thank you.

DAWN steps out of the light as FAWZIYA comes in. FAWZIYA is wearing her Jilbab again. She's nervous too…

FAWZIYA: Well. Okay. To start. Banned in French schools? All religious clothing is banned in French schools. No crosses, no Stars of David, no Jilbabs and absolutely no Virginity Rings. Actually, like, em, the real reason for this ban is that it was orchestrated by a Muslim – me – and the school was tarring us – me – with the terrorism brush. They said a religious assembly would cause unrest. Well there's been a hundred Christian assemblies but when one comes along that teaches the purity and the chastity and the respect for women so cherished by Islam, and all spearheaded by a

Muslim girl, it's banned. What a coincidence. It's my belief that this is a breach of my educational charter.

The buzzing gets a bit louder. FAWZIYA steps back and DAWN reappears. She looks smarter now. She's has a bit more conviction too. Louder. Time's passing quickly – montage style. There are a few people with DAWN this time, applauding her speech firmly…

DAWN: This is a breach of my Human Rights! I'd like to know one simple thing, what's the difference between their religious clothes and ours? Eh? Eh?

FAWZIYA now. She too has a small crowd with her and she speaks into more than one microphone. Her confidence has grown too…

FAWZIYA: Ours is a condition of faith and theirs is just an added extra. It's a sweetener for the real, more complex issue at the heart of this, something that is far closer to Islam than Christianity.

Big cheers as she steps away.

DAWN appears quickly, bigger and excited, as if she's addressing a large crowd. There's more folk with her now and they're agitated, jostling a bit. With an Obama-esque oratory flourish…

DAWN: Aye right!

Touché. Big cheers and jeers in equal measure. FAWZIYA's straight back, mob handed, but this time DAWN doesn't disappear. She faces FAWZIYA with her arms defiantly crossed. More and more outraged people arrive around them.

Cameras flash and huge TV lights shine unnaturally from all sides.

FAWZIYA: All we're doing is defending accusations from the Christian right. They started this!

DAWN: The Miracle Man is a Christian organisation of course we started it!

FAWZIYA: He preaches from a neutral perspective, read the website!

DAWN: I don't need to read the website, I've done the course! I've completed The Pathway unlike you!

FAWZIYA: These people have an agenda outside the realm of teenage health issues! We're the ones that are open to the rings and we want the rings, if it brings the pan-religious, non-denominational message of the Miracle Man to the school, and not as a sop to US-based extremists.

A police cordon now separates the two jostling, chanting crowds, which is a good thing cos they're wildly provoking each other. A big-time riot isn't far away. It's hard to hear the girls at the mic now so megaphones are handed forward.

DAWN: This is religious persecution so it is!

FAWZIYA: This is illegal!

DAWN: This is going to the courts!

FAWZIYA: This is going to the streets!

Banners appear with slogans like "Healy Hates Human Rights!", "Religious Equality Now!", "What Wouldn't Jesus Do?", "Death To Blasphemers!", "God is Great And So To A Lesser Extent Is The Miracle Man."

DAWN: We want rings! We want rings!

FAWZIYA: We want rings! We want rings!

Both crowds take up the chant and quickly swamp the girls.

In fact, as the protests move towards each other, it's impossible to see either FAWZIYA or DAWN in there at all as they are jostled and forgotten in the melee.

***

In his office. Mr HEALY sits with his head on his desk. The chanting crowd is clearly heard outside his window.

There's a tap at the door and OZZY comes in sheepishly.

OZZY: You wanted to see me Mr Healy?

HEALY: *(Lifting his head. Extremely calm.)* Did I? Did I really?

OZZY: Em…well, there was a message in my pigeon hole. It's a bit scrawled but…

HEALY: Oh I wonder what that could be about Mr MacDonald? Mm. Let me think. Nope. It's gone. Couldn't've been very important eh? Tell you what, you toddle along back to the staff room and if whatever it was occurs to me throughout the morning I'll give you a wee buzz, okay?

OZZY: Oh. Em. Okay.

HEALY: Okaydoaky then. Cheeribye.

OZZY: Cheeribye.

OZZY goes to leave, a bit confused.

HEALY: Oh no wait a minute. I remember now. It's nothing really. A silly thing actually. No, I wanted to have a wee word with you about the fact that you have, single-handedly, RUINED MY FUCKING LIFE YOU FUCKING ARSEHOLE!

OZZY: Oh. That.

HEALY: Aye, that! They are burning effigies out there! Fucking effigies! Of me! And they're lifelike. The one they were stamping on last night had wrist joints. I ask you, why go to the trouble of giving an effigy wrist joints only to stamp it to death on Scotland Speaks? Where are they getting them from, that's what I want to know? It's been ten bonfire nights since I've seen a decent Guy in a bogey, but oh, when there's an effigy needed, everyone's a fucking Blue Peter presenter.

OZZY: This is about The Miracle Man protests?

HEALY: Are you taking the piss? Look at this, *The Herald*: "Head Teacher Sparks Religious Row"; *The Scotsman*:

"Teacher Inflames Racial Tension"; *The Daily Record*: "Fascist Sir Virgin Fury". Fascist? How am I a fascist? If it was up to me I'd destroy anyone that believed in anything. If that makes me a fascist then I'm sorry.

OZZY: Actually I think that does...

HEALY: Bloody rings! Ya fucking...bastard. I literally can't win. If I don't have the show I'm restricting their rights, persecuting one faith in favour of another, and if I do I'm inflaming a public security issue. "God forbid we forbid God". Know who said that?

OZZY: Yeah.

HEALY: Wonder what he'd say if he could see you now eh? Look I'm not against people believing in stuff that's not true – each to their own. But keep it to yourself. That's just basic manners. Anyone who's decided to follow the teachings of Marvel comics, or believe in ghosts or the Loch Ness monster, they don't cause any trouble cos they're not trying to shove it down everyone's throat all the time. Give them their due, the Loch Ness guys are out there, in the pouring rain, hunting for evidence, get me? They're not just sitting back going "oh my dad told me it's true, and his dad told him, and he read it in a book so case fucking closed". They're not trying to change the way we live and alter the laws of nature just so they get the upper hand are they? Well are they?

OZZY: Who?

HEALY: The Loch Ness guys!

OZZY: What Loch Ness guys?

HEALY races to the window, slides it open and screams out to the crowds...

HEALY: It's a fiction!!!! It's fictional!!!

Unbelievably that gets a bad reaction. Cameras flash. He flops back down at his desk. After a moment...

HEALY: And I tell you what else gets me. These pricks: these screaming, effigy waving, arsehole war-starters…they've got absolutely no sense of humour. Noticed that? And that gets to me. Cos see me, I like a laugh.

Long pause.

OZZY: Will that be all?

HEALY: "Will that be all"?

OZZY: Should I go?

HEALY: "Will that be all? Should I go?" No, Ozzy. A resounding no to both of those enquiries. You started this shit-storm and you're going to bloody well finish it. I was at my lowest ebb for a while there, I admit it. I was having taboo thoughts – maybe it was time to jack it all in and go and work for the Inspectorate. Unthinkable stuff. But thankfully someone stepped up. I was actually in the process of booting him out when he told me his plan and it's a corker. As he says himself, he's a do-er. He's a man of action. History is made by people like him. *(Into the intercom.)* Morag send in that wee fat idiot will you? *(Back to Ozzy.)* See the genius bit is that it won't be religious. Not in the slightest. And if it's not religious we can hand out rings like we're bloody British Telecom; they just can't wear them in school. This way we can denounce this whole protest shebang as the work of extremists and move on. It's perfect actually.

OZZY: What is?

CHUBB swaggers in. He still has the neck brace on.

CHUBB: Mr Healy. Ozzy. How's the back? By the way I've prepared a wee apology especially for you. It's part of my plea bargain with the local authority but you'll have to wait cos it's in song form, and to do it justice I really need a beat.

HEALY: Need a beating more like. What did I say would happen if you kept talking your nonsense?

CHUBB: You said you'd kick my skull up.

HEALY: I'll kick it right up. And it would make my day Tubster so keep it coming, please. *(To Ozzy.)* This is him. Before you say anything, I know. But the idea is a good one. *(To CHUBB.)* Right go.

CHUBB: *(Clears throat.)* Ready? We have…our own Miracle Man show! It would be almost identical to the real one, give or take the odd compromise to avoid legal difficulties, but in essence it would be the same as theirs, except home-knitted.

HEALY: Not religious see? We're having the show, giving the headcases what they want and we haven't blinked in the process. Everyone's a winner.

OZZY: A home-knitted Miracle Man?

CHUBB: "Mirror-cool Man" it'll be.

OZZY: And what do Fawziya and Dawn say to this?

CHUBB: Don't know. They've got their own…agenda at the minute. I couldn't go along with them cos I'm changed. But I think they'll be happy cos some of these guys that have thrown their hat in are scary biscuits. They'll be glad to get rid I reckon. Rita's brother and that once got a play stopped in Birmingham.

HEALY: Ach so what? I stopped a pantomime once when I was six but you don't hear me going on about it. Nah, this'll make everything sweet, trust me.

CHUBB: And everyone will be friends again. *(To HEALY.)* Won't they?

HEALY: Absolutely. I'm sure after this you'll be very, very popular.

HEALY rolls his eyes behind CHUBB's back, for OZZY's benefit.

couldn't speak, they had to cut it and try again. But if you think about it, he's demanding the appearance of an evangelical Christian virginity show. Don't you think that's just a wee bit…odd?

DAWN: That's nothing. One of The Triple M Foundation gave me a print out of sexual practices that are allowed by the Bible and ones that are allowed by the Koran. I'm supposed to go out there, list them and say that the Bible lets you do more exciting stuff. I wish we could just run away man.

FAWZIYA: We can't, we started this.

DAWN: You started it you mean, it was your idea to kid-on we'd fallen out and start a war.

FAWZIYA: I didn't know it would come to this though! I thought: we put two sides against each other and good would prevail, the end. But now look. I can't believe he's gone! This is a nightmare. These people are a nightmare.

DAWN: I hate him the worst though. The Miracle Man. I hate him worse than all of them cos he was the one that wasn't going to let me down. Even if he didn't make it to the school he was supposed to be good and do the right thing and look after me but he didn't. Of course. Cos in real life people don't do that. Any of them. They finger folk and piss off instead. *(Beat.)* It was great for a while though, wasn't it? Not just cos it was brilliant for winding up Fiona Grant and getting on telly, but it was ace having someone like him kind of…there, wasn't it? Don't tell anyone Fawziya, right, but…he was my hero. Dumb eh? But now…I dunno…it's like he's transformed. Just like Fiona transformed. Or Dad when he left. Heroes? Aye right.

Pause.

FAWZIYA: My dad wrote me a letter after seeing me on the internet. It's…well…a bit confused. I think I might skip the trip over there until he calms down a wee bit. Mum's over the moon. She thinks I'm doing this to expose both sides as hysterical hypocrites, but honest to god, I'm not. That just happened.

DAWN: Here, talking about mad letters, Rita's brother's changed his tune. He's sending me threats now. It's out of order Fawziya. Your mob's getting scary.

FAWZIYA: Well yours got me surrounded in the street and sang a song about how I wasn't really a virgin cos me and Robert were shagging. Talk about scary.

DAWN: They did not say that. They said you were shagging Chubb.

FAWZIYA: That's the same guy.

DAWN: Oh aye so it is. *(Beat.)* God. Sorry. I am though. I'm totally, totally sorry.

FAWZIYA: Yeah. Me too.

There's a big cheer from onstage, followed by some angry shouts and heckling. The girls go closer to the wings to listen. We can hear bits of the debate, but it's not clear; just a rabble.

FAWZIYA: We did this for all the right reasons didn't we? We did this for good reasons. But it's all falling through the floor. *(Beat.)* You know what we should do? We should go out there and tell the truth. Tell the world that we faked our fall-out to steer public opinion. Then once we've apologised, and both sides have settled their differences, we can explain The Miracle Man's message of abstinence and healthy living in clear, reasonable terms. We'll do it together. If we do that I believe – I firmly believe – that good will prevail in the end.

DAWN: Yeah. Or we could just say fuck it and run away.

FAWZIYA: Yeah that is better – go!

They bolt.

When they're gone the onstage debate boils over into what sounds like a cowboy bar fight.

***

There's a transformation in progress…

The school gym starts empty and echoing; all wall-bars and pulled nets, basketball hoops and crash mats; but is slowly stripped and morphs into a school-made stage set for their very own Miracle Man.

The stage appears: high, rickety and oddly dipped in the middle.

A backdrop: all school play spangles and "Mirror-cool Man" lettering.

HEALY is walking OZZY through his ideas for the show. HEALY is wearing his director's hat – metaphorically and literally. CHUBB is taking notes.

HEALY: So my Vote of Thanks shouldn't take too long. Ten to fifteen minutes. A bit about fire safety and then boom! The show starts.

OZZY: Why can't the show just start? I think I'd prefer just to get it over with.

HEALY: What without a Vote of Thanks? How can a show start without a Vote of Thanks? What kind of show is that?

CHUBB: A good one.

HEALY: Pardon me Roland?

CHUBB: My name isn't…

HEALY: Your name is whatever I say it is. Don't think I've forgotten about the cost of that guttering. Right, I'm willing to negotiate on the fire safety but the Vote of Thanks stays. I'm famous for my Vote of Thanks. My Vote of Thanks at the Rotary Club was so good it actually got a Vote of Thanks. Unprecedented. No, a truly inspirational Vote of Thanks will add considerably to what we've already got. Trust me.

OZZY: Aye but what we've already got is... *(Trails off.)*

HEALY: Didn't catch the end of that.

CHUBB: Pish, he was going to say. He was making a pish shape with his mouth.

HEALY: *(To CHUBB.)* Swear again son and I'll scorch the earth from under you – starting with your UCAS forms.

CHUBB: But...

HEALY: Swearing is for the desperate. Write that down. And anyway, you're just being negative. Okay Mr MacDonald's a bit...stiff, but see tomorrow, once he gets an audience in front of him, the adrenaline will surge in his blood and he'll fly. Sinatra was much the same.

OZZY: All I'm saying is we've no lasers, no chain saws, no gospels choirs, no special effects, no nothing. It's already quite different to the original show.

HEALY: It has to be different for legal reasons.

OZZY: I know but...

HEALY: We've got a suitcase full of rings haven't we? Okay they're from Argos, but they're still rings. Plus, and it kills me to say this, the Techy department have done a top notch job on the stage. The Miracle Man himself couldn't tell the difference.

OZZY: Apart from the fact it dips in the middle.

CHUBB: And makes weird creaks.

HEALY: That's just it settling. Stages need time to settle, ask anyone. Oh, and have yous seen this? *(Shouting off.)* Lower it in Morag! Morag! Lower it in! Talk about special effects. This is awesome.

A massive, steel-framed, extremely heavy looking luminous cross drops in from above, raked at a very unusual angle. They move under it to get a better look.

HEALY: That is awesome. That is absolutely awesome.

OZZY: What is it?

HEALY: What is...What does it look like? It's the luminous cross for the finale?

CHUBB: How come it's all squinty?

HEALY: Legal requirements. And anyway, what's so weird about a squinty cross? Need I remind you that the flag of this great nation is a squinty cross. No, this fits the bill bang on: like the original but not religious. Plus it ripped the Techy's knitting getting it to hang like that, which was a nice wee bonus. A squinty cross won't kill anyone. And neither will a Vote of Thanks so they're locked. The details aren't important here. That said, I'm changing the details of your opening speech.

OZZY: What? No, I've learned it. It's nearly two pages long, I was up all night.

HEALY: Well tough luck DeNiro, it's getting changed. We were being too respectful to the real Miracle Man, which was fine back in the day, but seeing as now he's a sex offender we really should keep our distance. You know Ozzy if you're going to survive you'll have to be up for making some changes.

That hits OZZY hard. It's just what he was thinking. He doesn't take part in this next exchange...

CHUBB: And did yous hear? The net says that his magic heart was just coral. It was implanted under the skin and grew on the bones of his ribs. Cool eh?

HEALY: A coral heart? Yeah, that is pretty cool. How did it fasten on?

CHUBB: It grows on.

HEALY: No, I mean at first. It doesn't immediately grow on, it would have to graft on over time. I'm a biology teacher son, I think I know a little bit about coral implants.

CHUBB: Maybe the skin holds it in?

HEALY: Holds in coral? No way. No they must clip it on. Glue it on maybe.

CHUBB: Well. I dunno.

HEALY: Find out will you?

CHUBB: How will I find that out?

HEALY: How do you find anything out – Google it.

CHUBB: Now?

HEALY: Not now. We're doing the run-through now.

CHUBB: Well when then?

HEALY: Why are you resisting this?

CHUBB: I think it's an irrelevance.

HEALY: Who bloody cares what you think ya lazy little…

OZZY has moved away, rubbing his face.

OZZY: *(Interrupting.)* No. Look. No. No. I'm sorry. I can't. I'm not doing it.

HEALY: I'm not asking you to do it, I'm asking him to do it.

OZZY: Not that. Everything. The show. The Miracle Man. I'm not doing it. I can't. I can't do it. It's not me. People keep… yeah, yeah okay I started it rolling, maybe, probably, but I'm not the one to stop it. I can't. I'm not strong Mr Healy. I'm not. I'm not well.

HEALY: Ach that's just nerves. Two fingers down the gullet and you're hunky dory – that's the Sinatra way. This is all natural, trust me.

OZZY: No. *(Puts his hand to his chest.)* It's really not.

CHUBB: And look Ozzy don't worry about nerves. I've the very thing for this precise occasion: Reblin's Helmet of Ultimate Power! I've got no use for it now. My questing days are done. Here…bung that on and you'll feel like a different man.

CHUBB produces something from his back pocket and hands it over. OZZY looks at it for a moment and then puts on the "helmet". It's a balaclava.

CHUBB: You feel better don't you?

OZZY: Actually…I do. A little bit.

CHUBB: I know. You feel like someone else. Its magic is strong.

OZZY: I have to tell you something.

OZZY starts to unbutton his shirt. Before he can get to his second button though FAWZIYA and DAWN enter. OZZY stops when he sees them.

HEALY: *(To the girls.)* Hey! This is a closed set! No mobiles, no visitors, no interruptions! How did you get past Morag at the door?

DAWN: She's all tangled up in cables.

HEALY: Again? Why the hell does she keep tangling herself up in cables?

FAWZIYA: How's it going Robert?

CHUBB: Ozzy's bricking it, the stage is still to settle and we've got nothing much of anything except a Vote of Thanks.

HEALY: And rings.

CHUBB: And a squinty cross.

HEALY: More than enough to appease the zealots – so tell your troops to chill it. They wanted a Miracle Man they'll

get a Miracle Man and ours isn't even a sexual deviant
– despite current appearances. It's exactly what both sides
asked for. To the letter. Except the spelling. Pass that on
will you?

FAWZIYA: Well. That's why we're here. See, things have
changed.

DAWN: We've absconded and they've merged.

FAWZIYA: Not all of them have merged. Most of them have
just lost interest and gone home. Which is something to
celebrate really.

HEALY: Sorry, merged?

DAWN: Rita's Brother and Tabitha from the Triple M. They've
started a splinter group. They're called The Vigilant Pure
and they're...well, how would you describe them?

FAWZIYA: Mental?

DAWN: Aye, they're mental. They put out a statement saying
that they're united in their violent quest to destroy you and
your pagan corruption of the youth of Scotland. I've got
the threats here look.

She hands the letters to HEALY.

HEALY: Sorry, merged?

FAWZIYA: We've got nothing to do with it Sir. We abandoned
ship before this all kicked off. And we're also like, really
sorry.

DAWN: We are. Really sorry. But if you want, we can help
steer public opinion in your direction. Maybe tell folk
Ozzy has magic powers or something, get a bit of a freak
show vibe going.

FAWZIYA: Might be a bit late for that.

CHUBB: So, to recap…extreme Christians and extreme Muslims have united with a single purpose: to reek vengeance upon our very own Mr Healy?

FAWZIYA & DAWN: Yeah.

CHUBB: Wow. That is quite an achievement. *(To HEALY.)* You should be extremely proud Sir.

HEALY finds a seat, slowly sits and puts his head in his hands. There's a big pause.

OZZY: Will we be having the show if there's been threats made to…?

HEALY: No of course we won't be having the bloody show! The whole point of it was to…you can't put pupils in…

OZZY: So I'm not the Miracle Man?

HEALY: No. You're not the Miracle Man. No-one is.

PAULA enters. She's rushed over from the hospital, coat on.

PAULA: Excuse me, the woman in the cables said that… *(Sees OZZY.)* Oh my God.

OZZY: Paula?

PAULA: Ozzy? Why are you…? I couldn't get through on your mobile and they wouldn't pass on a message.

OZZY: What is it?

PAULA: Can I speak to you in private?

OZZY: What is it though? The tests?

PAULA: Please.

After a beat, OZZY nods, turns and exits across the "stage". PAULA follows him off.

HEALY: *(Weary.)* People just walking in and out. Strangers from the street, "oh aye come on in! It's fine. I mean we're only at Defcon 4 here. I'm only a legitimate target of international terrorism, it's no bother" Nobody cares of course. Why would they? *(Sigh.)* I'd better go and untangle Morag I suppose. Get the word out that the show's off and because of me, religious tension across the globe is just that little bit worse.

HEALY exits, shaking his head, starting to open and read the threats.

CHUBB: So tell us the truth. Is the only reason you abandoned the cause and came crawling back because you missed me?

DAWN: Who?

CHUBB: Both of you. You're both in love with me aren't you?

Both Girls. What? No way. Shut up. Gadz. Etc etc...

CHUBB: *(To FAWZIYA.)* What not even you?

FAWZIYA: I...I...I'm not in love with you.

CHUBB: *(Seriously.)* Just my body you want is it?

FAWZIYA: No! Oh my God. I would never...eeeew.

DAWN laughs. FAWZIYA can't help but smile a wee bit, despite herself. CHUBB laughs too.

CHUBB: Don't know why I'm laughing. *(Pause. Seriously.)* Poor Ozzy eh?

FAWZIYA: What is it do you think?

CHUBB shrugs.

***

"Backstage" in the gym. Actually it's OZZY's tiny office, but the PE and teacher stuff is swamped by props and costumes for the show: cardboard crosses and tin foil Stars of Davids, giant swords and angels wings and god knows what else. You could probably find, if you were really, really looking, a food groups poster ripped to bits and a strong man's costume crammed on a hanger. There is also a

lot of smashed stuff strewn about too: shattered coffee cups, broken rulers etc. There's a punch mark in the plaster.

OZZY is still wearing the balaclava. PAULA shuts the door behind her.

OZZY: Make it

Make it there's this guy. And this guy's dad is dying – everybody says so. And even though he never really got on with his dad he goes to the hospital every day. Because that's what you do.

And he even tells people that he's trying to help his dad. He tells people…he tells this one person, that he's making up stories in the hope that these stories will bring him back to life. His dad was a writer see. This guy's not a writer. This guy's nothing. But he tells her that he hopes the stories will help.

But it wasn't really true. In his heart…

See. In his heart he hopes the dad'll die. Because it's awful living with him. The fact that his dad is dying makes living – just simple day to day living – impossible. And he can't stand it anymore.

So he wishes him away. Secretly. Whisper, whispered it, in his heart. And he tells the stories because he knows his dad will hate it. Absolutely hate it. He'll hate hearing every dumb word coming from this guy's mouth. And the wish is, that he'll hate it so much that eventually he'll give up and go.

But that wish, that tiny black, bad, bad, wish, can't stay hidden. It can't. It grows into a heart where the whole world can see it. A broken heart. And that broken heart slowly fills with his dad's cancer.

He takes the cancer from his father. Takes the death from him. That's what he gets. And it serves him right.

This guy's had it coming.

Pause.

PAULA: That's not the story.

OZZY: Isn't it?

PAULA: Take that thing off.

OZZY: It's for the show. I'm someone else now.

PAULA: Take it off. And I'll tell you the real story.

Eventually he does. When she's sure he's listening...

PAULA: Make it there's this guy. A guy who's waiting on test results. Tests results, that when they come will come from a doctor by the way, not from a nurse in a room full of fancy dress.

And for all we know the results might be fine. Or they might be bad. But even if they are bad this guy will be be strong. Not because he's a strong man. Although he is. He'll be strong because everyone is strong. Even if they don't think it possible at first. They think it will be a miracle if they can make it through that very first night.

But they do. Even the ones who blame themselves for an accident that wasn't their fault years and years ago. Even the ones who hate themselves. They make it through the first night. And they make it through the next night too. And the next night and the next night.

They're strong because other people need them to be strong. I know. It sounds incredible doesn't it? Actually laughable when you try to put yourself in their place. But I've seen it. I see it every day. Everyone...everyone fights. In their own way. They hold it at arms length longer than you or I can believe. Longer than possible. But the strength just comes when it's needed. I promise. And more often than you can imagine, people survive.

Ozzy I don't know if you've got cancer. You might. But I know that Lewis has. And he's fought it and fought it. But in the next hour…he's going to die. That's why I'm here.

You have to come with me pet. Okay? You have to.

PAULA holds her hand out and OZZY takes it. There's a bit of noise off. HEALY's voice. Frantic sounding. It doesn't really register on PAULA or OZZY who exit hand in hand.

***

Back in the gym hall. HEALY has FAWZIYA, DAWN and CHUBB up on the stage. HEALY is freaking out. The rest don't seem too concerned. OZZY and DAWN enter back on to the stage…

HEALY: *(To OZZY.)* Don't move! Stay exactly where you are.

PAULA: We have to go. It's personal.

HEALY: You can't go, that's what I'm saying – the school's set to blow. *(The letter.)* It's a bomb threat! *(To the girls.)* You could've told me it was a bloody bomb threat.

DAWN: It's not really but. He never does half the things he says he's going to do. I've been waiting on his hand coming through the post for a month now. I'm like that, aye right.

FAWZIYA: We should just give the letter to the police Sir. I'm sure it's just a hoax to scupper the show.

CHUBB: Shouldn't we set off the fire alarm or something?

HEALY: Yes! Do that. No! That's what they would expect us to do. Maybe the fire alarm is the rigged?

CHUBB: They've not rigged the fire alarm. People don't rig things in real life. Sir just go across to the main building, phone the cops and send everyone home.

HEALY: I can't go out there I'm the target. And don't make those faces yous are all next in line. *(To Paula.)* Except you. I don't know who you are.

FAWZIYA: I'll go. I'm not scared.

DAWN: No I'll go. They won't hurt me.

CHUBB: We could all go together. The V Team. One last noble charge. One last hurrah.

Pause. OZZY remembers something. And it looks like, during the rest of this, that he's struggling to get the details of that memory straight in his head. Trying really hard to work this out...

HEALY: No. No, it's me that should go. The captain goes down with the ship. I seem to remember someone saying that during the last inspection. Mr MacDonald you wait here and make sure nothing happens to them.

PAULA: He can't. He's coming with me.

HEALY: No, he's staying here to look after these pupils.

PAULA: I'm from the hospital and I'm saying he leaves now.

HEALY: Well I'm his boss and I'm saying he stays.

PAULA: *(Overlapping.)* His father is...

HEALY: *(Overlapping.)* He has a duty of care to these children...

PAULA: *(Overlapping.)* He has a duty of care to his father, and believe you me there is no time to be...

HEALY: *(Overlapping.)* You don't get to come in here...

PAULA: *(Overlapping.)* This is ridiculous I can't believe...

HEALY: *(Overlapping.)* I can't believe that you would come in here and...

This escalates – both talking over each other, raised voices and pointed fingers, but we can't make much out.

OZZY has moved away from them, still on stage though.

OZZY: I can't go.

They didn't hear him.

OZZY: Stop. *(They don't.)* STOP. *(They do.)* I can't. I can't go.

PAULA: Ozzy, there's no time…

OZZY: I know. That's…why. I think.

PAULA: What? Ozzy you've been by his bed every night, this is the very last…

OZZY: I can't.

PAULA: You don't have to do what he says.

HEALY: *(To Paula.)* Or what you say.

PAULA: It's not me saying…

OZZY: No, it's me. It's me. It's me saying it. I'm saying I can't go. I can't go from here. This is who I am. This is what I'm supposed to do.

PAULA: What? Why?

OZZY: I don't know. I…I…can't remember.

He holds his head as if trying to get all this clear in his mind.

There's a pause.

PAULA: Ozzy…

OZZY: Ssh.

Another pause. No-one knows quite what's going on. Finally CHUBB decides to do something…

CHUBB: Ach bugger this. There comes a time when a knight must make a stand!

CHUBB strides over to the fire alarm…

HEALY: Don't you dare touch that fir…!

Too late. CHUBB breaks the glass with his fist and the alarm goes off. It's like the school bell only muffled and morphing. Weird sounding. But...no bomb. CHUBB makes a "what did I tell you?" gesture.

There's a low creaking noise and a shudder.

Another weird noise. A snapping.

FAWZIYA: What's happening?

HEALY: Oh god! It's a bomb. It's a bomb!

PAULA: Ach don't be daft. Bombs don't sound like that. Bombs go boom.

There's a massive BOOM.

The stage shudders. They scream. They cling together.

The lights change unnaturally. OZZY looks calm, as if it's all becoming clear.

There's a pause...then...a low, rising, roaring thunder.

Then the fast, sharp, shot of a blast.

It shoves OZZY backwards, to the middle of the stage as if he's on wires.

He feels a quick agony in his chest. He pulls his shirt open.

The heart on his chest seems to shine, a nano-second flash, like a ring caught in light.

Another huge groaning creek, as well as some snapping and clanging noises. The stage shifts, pulling everyone to its centre, clustered around OZZY, pushing him backwards.

They scream again. And just as they are about to run or jump, they hear a whiplash from above that freezes them dead.

It's the cross.

OZZY: Oh yeah. I get it now.

And with a slow, horrible snap

It falls...

OZZY feels like he sees this in slow motion.

The massive cross slips and plummets down towards FAWZIYA, DAWN, CHUBB, and HEALY.

It should kill them.

But it doesn't.

Because OZZY catches it.

He puts his arms up, and catches this massive, impossibly heavy, florescent crucifix. And he holds it there, above their heads

With all of his strength.

He strains under an unimaginable weight, but the cross is held high.

The others move away from underneath him, forming an awestruck circle on the edge of the shuddering stage.

There's just time for a moment of stunned silence before the centre of the stage collapses completely, sending the rest of them flying and OZZY disappearing under the cross, into darkness.

***

OZZY is falling through the howling abyss.

Stars zoom past. He's plummeting down through hyperspace.

And he's loving it!

The G force blows back his hair and stretches his face into a wide, giddy grin. His clothes snap and billow. His shirt is blasted off of his back and flaps up into the darkness above him.

He looks like a skydiver.

And now we can see that he's not alone.

Falling beside him is LEWIS.

It takes a minute or two before OZZY realises he has company...

OZZY: Hiya dad.

LEWIS: Hiya son.

OZZY: We're falling.

LEWIS: That we are.

OZZY: Feels good.

LEWIS: Yes it does.

OZZY: Unless...unless we're going to suddenly hit the ground. That wouldn't be too good would it?

LEWIS: No. Not too good.

OZZY: I suppose we can't fall forever. Can we?

LEWIS: I don't know son. I suppose we'll see.

OZZY: Yeah. Or maybe we can choose? Maybe we can choose to fall and choose to land?

LEWIS: There's not always a choice.

OZZY: Oh aye. You mean fate?

LEWIS: No. Not really.

Pause.

OZZY: Dad?

LEWIS: Yes?

OZZY: I'm sorry. I'm sorry I said that I wanted you to die. I didn't really mean it.

LEWIS: Ach maybe you did. A little bit. Maybe you just wanted to get back at me eh?

OZZY: For what?

LEWIS: For everything. For all the shit I've done.

OZZY: Well…am I your son?

LEWIS: Yes.

OZZY: Really though. Not in some spiritual way, not grafted on, but biologically. Am I your flesh and blood?

LEWIS: Yes. When you were a baby it was like looking in a mirror.

OZZY: So it's Fingal.

LEWIS: No, he's mine too. Your Mum was talking shite. She was struggling with alcohol at the time you know.

OZZY: Yeah I know but…why would she…?

LEWIS: She was trying to hurt me. Or…I don't know. You'll have to ask her. But it was a bad thing. One of the worst things she ever did. She's a complicated woman.

OZZY: Dad?

LEWIS: Mm?

OZZY: Would you say that you loved me?

LEWIS: Listen, you can't imagine the force of my love for you. It could blast diamonds into shards. It could turn the old young again.

OZZY: Then why didn't you…?

LEWIS: Because I was a prick Ozzy. I was a self-obsessed, self-righteous, pampered, worshipped, terrified old prick. Love didn't change that. Love couldn't break the sarcophagus of Me, the iron maiden shell of prickness I lived in. I was good at one thing Ozzy, only one. Writing words on paper. Everything else I did squalidly. Barely. The meagreness of my day to day existence was balanced out only by the ferocity of my words on paper. Not by love. Son, do you understand what I'm saying?

OZZY: You're saying…that you were a prick.

LEWIS: Aye.

OZZY: I must have been very disappointing for you then. As your real son.

LEWIS: No! Not at all. And neither was your brother. You amazed me. You still do. I liked the stories by the way.

OZZY: Did you? Really?

LEWIS: They're good.

OZZY: *(Smiles. Then...)* Where's Fingal?

LEWIS: He's teaching English as a foreign language in Prague.

OZZY: Oh is he?

LEWIS: Yeah.

OZZY: Good for him.

LEWIS: He hates it. But he's alright. Teaching English as a foreign language is the last bit of a breakdown for most people. Things usually get better after that. He's on his way back. He heard about it on the news. He's going to take the wrap for the accident. But he's going to be disappointed. They'll be no charges for him to face.

OZZY: What about mum?

LEWIS: Oh she'll be in touch when the cash comes up, don't worry. You'll have your work cut out, but do me a favour will you? Try to keep her close. I think you can change her. I think you can. You've got heart enough for all of us. When she comes she'll be claiming to have written *Thomas The Rhymer* so get the lawyers in line.

OZZY: Did she though?

LEWIS: Ach...Probably.

OZZY: So you're a...

LEWIS: I'm no fake Ozzy. And neither are you. Just keep going son. Keep going. You're doing well. You're doing really, really well.

OZZY: Dad, I'm going to remember you just like this, if that's okay?

LEWIS: Yeah, that's okay.

OZZY: I'm going to miss you dad.

LEWIS: I'll miss you too son. If I said sorry would it help you I wonder?

OZZY: I don't know. You could try.

LEWIS: Ossian...With a heart so full of love it bursts from my chest to yours; with a soul so ripped for the father I never was; and with my last real words, I tell you this: I'm sorry.

Pause.

LEWIS: Here.

 LEWIS: takes off his wedding ring and hands it to Ozzy. Ozzy puts it on and realises...

OZZY: You can choose.

LEWIS: Can you?

OZZY: Yeah. Bye dad.

LEWIS: Bye son.

OZZY spreads his arms wide like wings and stops falling.

His father continues to drop, disappearing down and away. OZZY flips over so that he's now floating on his back.

And then, with a soft bounce

He lands.

***

We can see now that OZZY is lying in a darkened hospital room, the stars are just the blinking lights on the equipment hooked up to his bed.

He wakes. He turns to where his dad was a second ago.

There's an empty bed beside him.

He looks down at his hand. He's wearing his father's wedding ring.

PAULA is sitting beside him. She takes his hand.

PAULA: He didn't suffer pet. His breathing slowed down. Slower and slower, quieter and quieter until there was no more breath to come. And then he was gone. All the lines left his face and he didn't wake. You were right beside him after all.

OZZY: I know. What happened?

PAULA: Well, the pain control eventually overtakes the system…

OZZY: No. I mean what happened to me?

PAULA: Don't you remember?

OZZY: Not really.

PAULA: You saved everyone. It was on the news. You were like a superhero or something. No-one could've held that weight. It was steel. It was a miracle. To have that kind of strength. There's been journalists camped out in the coffee bar all night. Not just because of Lewis, but because of you. *(Pause.)* Ozzy… Listen. A doctor is going to speak to you.

OZZY: About the tests?

PAULA: Aye.

OZZY: It's okay. I'm ready now.

Pause.

OZZY: Paula? My dad's dead.

PAULA: I know.

OZZY: I feel like I'm…a little kid.

PAULA: So do I. Sometimes. It's awful lonely isn't it?

OZZY: Yeah.

PAULA: Yeah. And you wish someone would cradle you and just…cradle you.

OZZY holds PAULA's hand and pulls her towards him. They kiss. She lies on the bed beside him.

OZZY: I'll cradle you.

***

Mr HEALY is addressing the media…

HEALY: It is my understanding that our colleague, teacher and great friend, Mr Ossian MacDonald, while recovering in hospital and grieving for his illustrious father, would wish me to undertake any media duties regarding what I believe is being referred to as "The Miracle Man Incident". This world, of cameras, interviews and celebrity introductions, is a new one to me and although some have been kind enough to say that I'm rather gifted in this department, I must say before we begin, that to be perfectly honest with you, I'll be glad when I can return to my daily, humdrum, tedious, headmastering duties.

Em…update…The school has imposed a blanket ban on absolutely all jewellery in light of an incident on Thursday where a boy had a finger partially severed after a ring he was wearing, his father's wedding ring I believe, was caught in the collapsing stage. Luckily a nurse was on the scene to save the finger which I'm told he uses regularly.

Health and safety governs this decision, not, and I hope this will be clear, any religious or political ideology. To prove this point I am also banning balaclavas.

As far as the stage collapse, there is absolutely no evidence of terrorist activity, despite a group called The Vigilant Pure taking responsibility. This group, comprising of only two people, have been ruled out as a serious threat to anybody except themselves. In fact, all evidence seems to show that the stage's construction was at fault from the very first and was at no point fit for performance. I fully stand by our technical department, who built the stage, and will be shoulder to shoulder with them during any witch-hunt which may or may not seek to discredit and humiliate them in the weeks, months and years to come. However at this point, I'm glad to say, as far as the school is concerned, everything is back normal. Neither better, nor indeed, worse.

Any questions?

The flash of the cameras and the crush of microphones indicate that to HEALY's delight, yes, there are.

***

FAWZIYA and DAWN are standing in a park. Apart from FAWZIYA's headscarf, they are wearing identical tracksuits and trainers.

CHUBB arrives with his arm in a sling. He has a bag with him.

DAWN: What kept you?

CHUBB: What kept me? Medicine's finest can't believe I'm out my pit at all, never mind running errands in parks for ungrateful swines.

FAWZIYA: Ah give us a break, you're fine.

CHUBB: Aye right. *(Holding up his hand.)* You understand of course if it wasn't for my hideous disfigurement I'd be joining you don't you?

DAWN: Just us girls I'm afraid.

FAWZIYA: You can give us a wave as we zoom by in a blur.

CHUBB: I think my waving days are over. How many names did you get in the end?

DAWN: 900.

CHUBB: 900! That's amazing.

DAWN: Fawziya got the folk in her mosque to sign up…

FAWZIYA: And I bow down to Dawn's miraculous powers of playground persuasion. Talk about steering public opinion? After that picture in the paper of her covered in blood and dust she could've got world peace if she'd wanted it: "Teenage Crash Hero Pleads For An End To Protests". Queen of the Playground!

DAWN: Shut up man! But I am.

CHUBB: 900 sponsors. You'll make a bomb. Oh aye, I've got your numbers.

CHUBB produces two bibs from his bag and the girls put them over their tracksuits.

The bibs say… "I'm Running For… Ozzy".

FAWZIYA: See you at the finishing line right Robert?

CHUBB: Yeah. But if it takes you hours I might dog it and get you at the meeting. What yous arguing about tonight?

DAWN: It's not argument, it's debate. A lively exchange of ideas on faith-based issues. It's the future.

CHUBB: So you keep saying. Right, good luck merry damsels and may your quest end in glory and riches for all charities concerned and not in cramp, twisted ankles or roadside vomiting.

FAWZIYA: Aw get lost Robert!

DAWN: Aye see you later Chubb!

CHUBB: Good luck though. I mean it. First one past the finishing line gets to be my girlfriend.

FAWZIYA: Is that a serious offer?

CHUBB: Could be. How? Do you want it to be a serious offer?

FAWZIYA: Dunno. Do you want that I would want it to be a serious offer?

CHUBB: Depends. Do you want that I want...

DAWN: Oh for God sake quit it with that crap. Gives me the boak.

FAWZIYA: Catch you later Robert.

CHUBB: Hope so.

CHUBB smiles, waves and heads off.

A banner appears above them. It says "CANCER RESEARCH UK: RACE FOR LIFE".

DAWN: Remember what we said. We'll start together...

FAWZIYA: And we'll end together, I know.

DAWN: Don't want you sprinting off and leaving me.

FAWZIYA: Believe me. That's not going to be an issue. Have faith.

The girls are slowly surrounded by a crowd of women.

A voice is booming out "Ladies: It's time to Race For Life. On your marks, get set... GO!"

And they're off.

All of these people – constellations of people – running to raise money, to do something.

All of them wearing a number with a name on it.

And maybe that's the name of a person they're trying to save.

Because sometimes people save other people. Don't they?

Or maybe it's the name of a person who's already gone, and this is a grand gesture, a kind of prayer really.

Or maybe it's something else.

Because, if you look closely, some of these runners are wearing bibs that say

"I'm running for…myself".

The End

www.ingramcontent.com/pod-product-compliance
Ingram Content Group UK Ltd.
Pitfield, Milton Keynes, MK11 3LW, UK
UKHW020724280225
455688UK00012B/488